Grant Writing Tips for Nurses and Other Health Professionals

Carole Kenner, DNS, RNC, FAAN
Associate Dean for Academic Advancement/Professor Clinical Nursing
University of Illinois at Chicago
President, Consultants with Confidence, Inc.
Past President
National Association of Neonatal Nurses
Buffalo Grove, IL

Marlene Walden, PhD, RNC, NNP
Former Special Interest Group Director at Large
National Association of Neonatal Nurses
Assistant Professor
Baylor College of Medicine
Texas Children's Hospital
Houston, TX

WASHINGTON, D.C.

Library of Congress Cataloging-in-Publication Data

Kenner, Carole.
Grant writing tips for nurses and other health professionals / Carole Kenner, Marlene Walden.
p. cm.
Includes bibliographical references and index.
ISBN 1-55810-173-X
1. Nursing–Research grants. 2. Proposal writing for grants. 3. Proposal writing in medicine. I. Walden, Marlene, 1956- II. Title.
RT73 .K46 2001
610.73'079—dc21

2001035292

Published by
American Nurses Publishing
600 Maryland Avenue, SW
Suite 100 West
Washington, D.C. 20024-2571

ISBN 1-55810-173-X

GWT21 1.5M 06/01

Acknowledgments

We would like to thank Rosanne O' Connor, Publisher, ANA Publishing, for her belief in this project and encouragement in developing this monograph.

We would also like to thank Janice Zasada with The In Bin Inc., for formatting, editing and typing this manuscript.

Eric Wurzbacher, Editor and Project Manager, ANA Publishing came in at the end of the project and helped us with the final revisions and edits. Thank you for your help in making this a wonderful resource.

This project grew out of a presentation done by Carole Kenner and Marlene Walden at a National Association of Neonatal Nurses conference.

Preface

Grant writing is an essential skill for nurses today. Yet it can be a daunting task to put fingers to keyboard and really formulate your grant. This monograph is a very informal conversation about the art and process of how to write grants with minimal frustration. At least we hope we accomplish that goal! The book is formatted to follow the basic steps of grant writing. The language is first person to get the reader involved in the process. Examples are given from each of the authors' experiences in this area. Most books on writing fundable grants are very detailed; dry with few experiences. We have attempted to cut to the chase and give you the bare bones and quick tips that a busy nurse, would-be grant writer, needs for this adventure.

Grant writing can be exciting and even profitable given the right tools. This book is one of the "right tools." Happy grant writing!

Carole Kenner, DNS, RNC, FAAN
Marlene Walden, PhD, RNC, NNP

Contents

So You Want to Write a Grant! Where to Begin 1

Many health professionals often perceive grant writing as overwhelming and intimidating, at best. As health care moves toward more evidence-based practice, staff nurses and practitioners at the bedside are often faced with the challenge of validating current therapies without the personnel or financial resources to do so. Managed care contracts are putting more and more pressure on providing cost-effective, outcome-based care. These corporations are calling for standardization of clinical protocols and treatment plans. Care maps are being used to benchmark processes in specific patient populations. The process of validating the effectiveness of current nursing and medical therapies is a concern of clinical staff as well as the academicians in health science centers.

In academia, faculty are also under great pressure to write grants to develop, revise, or expand their own programs of research or to write program training grants to meet changing student, institutional, or managed care demands that affect undergraduate and graduate education. In fact, for many faculty or project coordinators in health care settings, how successful one is at the art of grant writing often determines tenure status and/or continued employment at a particular academic or clinical institution. Thus, health care professionals across a diverse spectrum of positions require solid grant writing knowledge and skills that will enable them to be successful in an increasingly competitive funding market.

Although the process of grant writing is very time consuming, and at times all encompassing, taking on a life of its own, getting a grant funded is also very doable given the right idea and some basic grant writing skills. Breaking down the project into manageable pieces is often the key to success. This chapter will focus on how one determines how a grant needs to be written, sources by which to generate fundable ideas, and finally, how to know if you are asking the right question. Although many types of grants can be obtained, three of the most common include research, program, and special projects/demonstration grants. Examples in this chapter will primarily address the research grant, although the principles of grant writing may be applied to other types of grants.

Establishing the Need for a Grant

How one approaches the grant writing process will often determine not only how successful one is at it, but also how tolerable the experience will be. The need to write a grant may be as simple as the need to justify outcomes in a competitive managed health care environment. More commonly, however, grants are written for the purpose of expanding one's own program of research and gaining release time from clinical or classroom teaching responsibilities for scholarly activities. Academicians often seek training grants to expand or significantly revise the curriculum within a college or university while keeping costs down by hiring program faculty specifically on the grant monies. This strategy allows the school to demonstrate the self-sufficiency and success of the program during the first 3 years (program grants are usually 3 to 5 years in length) before assuming the total costs involved in a new program. A special projects or demonstration grant is normally used to facilitate the development of an educational or clinical program where no similar programs exist in a particular geographic area. Before the community will embrace the idea, funds must be obtained to demonstrate the efficacy of the program. For example, this strategy was used for the first school-based, nurse-run health clinics.

The need for writing a grant can be a professional choice, or it can be dictated by the employing institution. In either circumstance, writing a grant can often be very stressful for the individual involved. Having the self-determination and personal energy reserves necessary to survive the sometimes grueling grant writing process depends in large part on the commitment one has to the grant, the passion felt for the answer to the question, and the resources to assist in the process. One cannot and should not down play the many sacrifices that will have to be made to get the grant ready for a timely submission to an external funding agency. The sheer pressure of tight timelines and competing responsibilities when one is writing a grant has turned many "angelic" Dr. Jekyll colleagues into grant writing "terrors" resembling Mr. Hyde. These individuals tend to be unpleasant when they are in the midst of the grant writing process. Instead of thriving on the academic challenge of taking an idea and turning it into a fundable project, they often find themselves in the survival mode. But is the goal of grant writing survival, or can the individual actually thrive during the grant writing process?

Those individuals who approach grant writing in the survival mode are less likely to be successful in their efforts and certainly will make themselves, and perhaps others, miserable in the process. When not given a choice about writing the grant, the process often becomes arduous. However, when grant writing is approached in the "thrival" mode and is viewed as future possibilities and opportunities, the potentially burdensome task of writing can be transformed into an exciting intellectual adventure. The grant is the opportunity to answer that nagging clinical question or to develop a program or clinical project to meet an aggregate need. That is exciting. You are contributing to the body of scientific and theoretical knowledge.

Excitement about instead of the dread of the journey creates the energy and focus needed to sustain the process of grant writing. The choice to survive or thrive in writing a grant is a personal one. Although jobs often depend on the task of grant writing, the individual has the option to view it as an arduous task or to be challenged about the opportunities and possibilities that the future holds for the successful grant writer.

Sources for a Fundable Idea

Developing a fundable idea takes ingenuity on the part of the grant writer. Ideas may come from a number of sources, both clinically and professionally. Some of the best ideas often arise from clinical practice. This clinical base has been the case in my own professional experience. When I entered neonatal nursing in the late 1970s, health care professionals in the Neonatal Intensive Care Unit (NICU) did not believe that preterm infants had the autonomic or functional capacity to perceive pain due to their immature central nervous systems. As a novice nurse, I looked to my medical and nursing colleagues to guide me in learning, to care for critically ill neonates. After seeing the hurt and hearing the cries, I became convinced that the current thinking about neonatal pain was inaccurate. This professional observation was the source for my own program of research and grant writing efforts. I could not, however, just go out and study neonatal pain. I needed equipment and personal resources. That is where grant writing fit into my research plans.

Regardless of which clinical area one practices, evaluating the research base of that practice is a source of many fundable ideas. Gaps in the literature or conflicting results from previous studies may be another source of ideas for research and, therefore, a grant. Questions that the literature has left unresolved are great avenues for future research and, depending on the research priorities of the various funding agencies, also great venues for external funding.

Attending professional conferences is another excellent source for research idea generation. One usually becomes energized at a conference and believes the world is conquerable. The power of networking with researchers in the field and talking with other health care professionals from around the country cannot be underestimated. Many researchers are anxious to replicate their studies in another setting or for their instruments to be retested. Both of these strategies add to their own database and research credibility. This replication provides novices a chance to use already developed and tested methods and data collection instruments. Use of nationally known experts on grants as project team members or consultants will increase the credibility of the grant application. Through such help and also through conference networking, becoming knowledgeable about what other researchers are doing in a particular field helps the grant writer to avoid duplicating current work or replicating errors. It allows the researcher to focus on a grant angle that has the potential for generating new knowledge or adding depth to existing knowledge. Furthermore, networking may also help to form collaborative relationships between individuals with similar interests. These interactions may help to strengthen an idea or may lead to ideas not previously considered.

Identifying mentors in the area, whether it be a research, training, or special projects grant, has many advantages. Involving a mentor not only allows the grant writer to utilize their expertise to develop the grant proposal, but may also set the stage for future collaborations. If these individuals are considered the experts in the field, the funding agency may ask them to review your work. Learning from the "master" as you shape your own ideas and educational or research program will be invaluable as will the relationship you establish.

Although strong attention to literature and colleagues within your own area of interest may lead to a plausible grant idea, pushing the envelope by exploring other related fields may also be productive as a source of idea generation. For example, if your area of interest was in pain in neonates, reading or attending conferences that deal with pain in children or adults may lead to a new assessment technique or pain management therapy that has not previously been extended to the neonatal population.

Another example of a related field that you could explore if you were interested in pain in neonates is molecular neurobiology. Expounding upon this example, parents of former preterm infants in the NICU often report high pain thresholds in their infants, for example, "My child does not exhibit the same level of pain as other children do when they fall down or touch a hot stove." These anecdotal reports by parents have also been substantiated in at least one study where the researchers report decreased pain sensitivity among former preterm infants who were now at a corrected age of 18 months (Grunau, Whitfield, and Petrie 1994). These observations, coupled with preliminary research findings, may stimulate the grant writer to explore new concepts within the field of molecular neurobiology. A fundable research question might deal with the molecular basis within the nervous system by which pain pathways are altered in preterm infants, thus providing a plausible explanation for why these children have higher pain thresholds than healthy infants born at term. Subsequent studies could then explore effective interventions to minimize the long-term effects of chronic, repeated pain in critically ill preterm infants.

Along the same lines, journal clubs may be a source of ideas for future grant writing. Meetings such as these often point to differences in care practices between health care providers from different institutions. They may also lead to the realization that the current research base is insufficient to support a current therapeutic regimen and thus support the need for further research in this area.

No matter what strategy you find helpful in generating ideas, it will be important at some point in this process to set aside time to think about all the information that you have gathered. One of the hindrances to the success of grant writers is busy schedules and other demands. In today's work setting, everyone is asked to work harder, often with fewer resources. Many times, by the end of the workday, you probably feel exhausted. Yet the work does not end there. Working at this level consistently promotes professional burnout and stifles creativity in your grant writing. Successful grant writers and researchers often emphasize the need to relentlessly protect time for scholarship. This dedicated time must fit your own work schedule and knowledge of how you best function. One day a week or even a couple of hours each day are two variations of dedicated writing time. The schedule is up to you. You determine whatever works for you. But whatever it is, just do it!

Is the Question the Right Question?

Determining whether the question is the right question takes considerable thought. Ideally, the right question is congruent with your own research interests. When you have a passion for the topic, you are more likely to have the perseverance to maintain your pursuit through the long, tedious grant writing process.

Although your passion for the topic is important, you will also need to ensure that your area of research is of critical interest to others. Because of the competitive nature of external funding sources, your area of interest needs to be broad enough so that it appeals to a sufficient target population to warrant funding. Funding agencies often set broad research funding priorities, with many using *Healthy People 2010* objectives. (See Appendix C for list of *Healthy People 2010* objectives). You will need to examine each of the potential funding agencies, determine their funding priorities, determine their individual rules for obtaining funds such as using your professional association membership to access members-only funds or having certain credentials, and choose the best match for your particular area of interest.

Tips for Dedicated Time

Try the following "tricks of the trade."

- I find it helpful to immerse myself for longer rather than shorter blocks of time.
- If you find yourself spending too much time figuring out where you left off when the writing is done in shorter work sessions, you might increase your productivity by scheduling longer sessions.
- You will also need to determine what kind of environment is needed to increase personal productivity. For some, it is a quiet environment free from distractions; for others, it might be the library.

In addition to a broad focus, give your idea a unique slant. Many times the specific slant of your question will need to be tailored more directly to the funding priorities identified. For example, the National Institute for Nursing Research (NINR) has an ongoing call out for proposals to improve the clinical management and care delivery for patients who require mechanical ventilation. If your area were pain management in neonates, you might choose to submit a grant proposal that details an intervention for providing caregiver containment during endotracheal suctioning procedures. This intervention has been demonstrated in a similar study in neonates undergoing a heel stick procedure to significantly reduce pain responses as well as promote shorter sleep disruption times (Corff, Seideman, Venkataraman, Lutes, and Yates 1995). As another example, if you are an adult hospice nurse you may want to look at comfort care for those patients who are in need of palliative care. This represents a broad focus. The next step would be to narrow the focus to a specific type of patient such as a young adult patients experiencing end-stage lung cancer.

Conclusion

Writing a great proposal starts with a great idea. Before starting to write any grant proposal, systematically review the literature, talk with experts in the field, and obtain consultations as necessary. Identify a question that is relevant, one that has the potential to generate new knowledge, solve a clinical management problem, or produce a new type of educational program. In addition, be sure it is broad enough to be of interest to a significant portion of the funding source's population. By taking the time to do your homework and find a match between your area of research and current funding options, you will substantially increase your success at obtaining grant monies.

What Type of Grant Do You Want? 2

Many types of grants are available to health care professionals. Some are limited by geographic area, membership in a professional organization, place of employment, or career level. Primarily these grants fall into six categories: foundation grants, hospital-based grants, professional association grants, corporate partnerships, pre- and post-doctoral fellowships, and federal grants.

Foundation Grants

Foundation grants are those that support the mission and goals of specific philanthropic societies. They may or may not have a specific funding cycle. Some foundations review grants when they are submitted. Others have timelines and guidelines for application. Certain health maintenance organizations and managed care groups now have foundations whose purpose is to support community projects to increase their visibility. Professional associations often create foundations to support their members; they are separate corporate entities from the parent organization. Membership, however, in the association is one criterion for grant eligibility. Foundations are likely to request a letter of inquiry or a brief synopsis of a project before requesting a full proposal.

Foundation grants are a nice way to start your attempts at funding. For most foundations, the submission process is fairly straightforward and brief compared to federal grants. They provide small sums of money for very specific focus areas. These funds are good as seed money to start projects. For example, in my own work I saw a call for the Purdue Friedrick Foundation via an Association Newsletter. Their areas of interest were perinatal health care. I submitted a brief proposal for a qualitative research study "Transition from Hospital to Home for Mothers and Babies." This research was my dissertation and I got funded within 3 months of submission. This seed money gave me a good start to then seek more funding for my next project that again focused on "Transition" research. My ability to successfully write a foundation grant gave me confidence that I could go on for other foundation monies as well as federal ones. The foundation grant process is less intimidating and usually provides a quick turnaround time for an answer to whether or not the project is fundable.

I used the March of Dimes Birth Defects Foundation of Greater Cincinnati to seek funds for a professional educational component of my Centers for Disease Control and Prevention (CDC)-funded Perinatal Alcohol Users grant. The foundation monies were to support an educational intervention aimed at increasing the awareness of health professionals about the harmful effect of perinatal alcohol use at any stage of the pregnancy. As a clinician, I, like other members of my research team, felt we were seeing more women delivering alcohol-exposed babies than the report rates reflected in our prenatal clinics. The aim of our research to include health professional education about potential harmful birth defects from perinatal alcohol exposure fit with the March of Dimes Birth Defects Foundation's goals. The first step in the application process was a letter of intent to ensure there was a fit between the project's specific aims and the foundation's mission. The March of Dime's Birth Defects Foundation's request for proposal was sent about 2 weeks following submission of our letter of intent. (See Appendix D.) We then submitted a full proposal. A positive funding decision was reached about 8 weeks after the proposal submission.

I have submitted grants to other foundations such as the Gates Foundation. The University of Cincinnati Colleges of Medicine and Nursing sent a grant proposal to this foundation. The purpose was to support education of faculty in Honduras in these two disciplines. The grant would provide for faculty exchanges and eventually student exchanges. The Gates Foundation seeks projects that are aimed at increasing the educational level (not just of health professionals) in third world countries. The application was very brief and required a concise synthesis of the project. The proposal's brevity was a challenge. The human tendency is to want to give a lot of information instead of a concise presentation. Therefore, in many respects the short grants can be more of a challenge than the longer ones although the process itself is less awesome.

Examples of foundations that provide grant opportunities include

- Kellogg Foundation
- Robert Wood Johnson Foundation
- Choice Care Foundation of Cincinnati, Ohio
- Pew Charitable Trusts Foundation
- March of Dimes Birth Defects Foundation
- Rockefeller Foundation
- Gates Foundation

Other foundations are associated with professional associations and will be discussed under that heading.

Hospital-Based Grants

Hospital-based grants generally are offered only to employees of their organizations. The hospital may request proposals for certain projects that they wish to see started. In the past, these grants were most likely to go to physicians simply because other health professionals did not know about their existence. These grants support small budgets and act as seed money for other facets or phases of the project. A wealthy donor may tie the funds to a specific type of research due to an endowment to the hospital. Other funds may be administered through a hospital foundation whose express purpose is to further any research that will enhance the health care of individuals served by the hospital.

Another positive aspect of partnering with a hospital is access to the patient population, especially if that is important in the research desired. The clinical agency has a need to provide sound clinical outcomes, but they do not always have the expertise at hand or the time to set up a research protocol. The academician on the other hand has the desire and often push from the reappointment and tenure committee to do research, but lacks the access to the clinical setting. So the "marriage" of the two institutions can benefit both parties.

A good example of a hospital-based grant came from a local hospital in Cincinnati that wanted to increase customer satisfaction of their inpatient obstetric patients. I had done research in the area of "Transition from Hospital to Home for Mothers and Babies." I had a master's student who wanted to do a part of my transition research as her thesis. We approached a Maternal Child Clinical Nurse Specialist (CNS) who worked at an area level II nursery. She was very anxious to make changes in their follow-up care for mothers and babies, but she needed evidence to support the need for more coordinated follow-up and teaching after discharge. We talked with her about our ideas. She told us of the funds her hospital provided for research. So within 2 months we wrote a proposal that served three purposes: extended my research to a new setting, gave my master's student a thesis, and gave the CNS an opportunity to gain support for her clinical ideas. Another aspect of this process was that all of us were gaining experience in grant writing. The proposal was very short and easy to write. The project was funded in a few weeks. For the master's student, she came out with a thesis and her first grant. She finished her study with a very positive feeling toward research. For the hospital, the basis for what would eventually become a home follow-up program that netted a profit and good public relations was created.

Professional Association Grants

Many professional associations offer grant opportunities to their members. These grants are either directly administered by the association or through an auxiliary foundation. Corporate sponsors of the association sometimes partner with the professional society to offer educational scholarships or research grants. For example, equipment companies that exhibit at medical conferences will also allocate monies to an association for the express purpose of testing protocol using their equipment. This type of grant would be a focused or targeted grant. Other associations such as the Oncology Nurses Association (ONS) have associated foundations that give seed monies once per year to grantees who want to conduct research in the areas targeted by the association.

Foundation grants may have a definite application deadline or a rolling deadline, which means they review grants whenever one is sent. The submission of these grants is sometimes preceded by a letter of intent (see Appendix D for a sample). This letter of intent describes in just a very few pages what the focus of the project will be. It allows the foundation reviewers to determine if in fact the project is within the scope of the foundation's mission. Then if the project is acceptable to the mission, the grant seeker will be asked to submit a full proposal according to specified guidelines.

As the nursing shortage has increased, so has the number of scholarships or foundation grants that are aimed at education. Foundation grants linked with nursing specialty associations will generally support research in the area of specialty focus or educational endeavors. The latter grant aims to increase the number of nurses in either the area of specialty focus or the nurses' level of education. The advantage to the foundation is to attract members to their parent association. Membership in the association is a prerequisite to the application process.

The American Nurses Foundation (ANF) is a good example of a foundation that will support research and special projects across nursing specialties. They partner with Sigma Theta Tau International for some of their grants. To apply for their grants you must be a member of the American Nurses Association (ANA). Therefore, the parent organization (ANA) wins by getting more members and ANF wins by increasing their visibility to attract more donors. Professional association grants represent nearly every nursing specialty. Some are not through a parent foundation but directly from the association itself. The following are just a few examples:

- Society of Pediatric Nurses (SPN) awards a $1,000 Corrine Barnes Research Grant
- International Society of Nurses in Genetics (ISONG) Nursing Research Small Grant Program
- American Cancer Society Targeted Grants for Research Directed at Poor and Underserved Populations
- American Association of Critical Care Nurses (AACN) Educational Advancement Scholarships for BSN Completion and Graduate Education
- National Association of Pediatric Nurse Associates and Practitioners (NAPNAP) Foundation Grants for nursing research that contribute to the improvement of quality of life for children and their families
- NAPNAP Graduate Student Research Award to support child and family research among graduate students

Corporate Partnerships

Corporate partnerships are often grants for research, product development, implementation, or evaluation. These partnerships or strategic alliances are forged directly with a researcher/educator, an academic institution, or as described above with a professional association. Many professionals view these with skepticism, because they are concerned that if the research findings do not support the company's view, they will be asked to change the findings or not report them. Although there is always an element of danger with some companies, the researcher or grant seeker, before signing on the bottom line, should find out what parameters must be followed for reporting, presenting, and publishing the data. In other words, who owns the data and who has the right to manipulate it? Those are important up-front questions that must be answered before any partnerships are forged.

A potential researcher who already knows a certain type of equipment or protocol that is to be used may seek corporate partnership grants. Seeking support from that company can make good sense for this type of partnership and can be a win-win arrangement for both parties as long as each party is clear about expectations of the research and the dissemination of the findings. If a researcher is interested in this type of relationship, then either the local sales representative for the company or the research and development department of the company is an appropriate contact. Many larger companies have at least one if not a whole department of people responsible for clinical research. Often the researcher can help the company gain entry to a clinical or academic setting that otherwise would be closed to them. Corporate grants can open up possibilities to do international, multi-site studies that in the past were difficult to perform unless the researcher had the right connections. Today, with the globalization of industry, the corporate world provides opportunities to use already established markets for their products as research sites. To a North American researcher, these corporations open international portals for multi-site research.

Examples of corporate partnership grants are:

- Children's Medical Ventures funds developmental care research, not just studies using their products
- MedImmune funds research regarding pharmacologic intervention with respiratory syncytial virus
- Roche U.S. Pharmaceuticals funds studies based on genomics (study of encoded information in DNA) that examines the sequence of infectious pathogens and drugs to combat them
- Parke-Davis along with The Canadian Pain Society funds chronic pain research

Pre- and Post-Doctoral Fellowships

Pre- and post-doctoral Fellowships are expressly for the education and training of those professionals interested in specializing in one area of research or education.

Most of these fellowships support part if not all the academic costs associated with moving into a higher level of education or research sophistication. Foundations, associations, or the federal government may grant these.

A *pre-doctoral fellowship* focuses on gaining further education and training for a person with a master's degree who is believed to want to go on for further research/education. It allows the professional to gain a new skill set to qualify competitively for leading doctoral programs. It is one way that academic institutions can groom professionals for a research or academic career and move them into the doctoral programs.

Post-doctoral grants are aimed at perfecting and honing already existing research skills. Generally, grants in these highly specialized areas of expertise are offered for 1 to 2 years of in-depth studies. Today, many of these have to do with bench (laboratory) research in the areas of pain, the human genome, and cancer treatments. Other hot topics are ethics, workplace analysis, health policy, and clinical scholarship programs.

The purpose of pre- and post-doctoral fellowships is to create a cadre of scholars across disciplines that will lead the health profession into the next millennium. The rapid growth of technology has made it essential to have experts who will set the direction and give vision to the profession. Examples of pre- and post-doctoral fellowship grants are:

- Pfizer Postdoctoral Fellowship Program in Biological Psychiatry
- National Research Service Award (NRSA) Training Grants and Fellowships:
  - Individual Predoctoral Fellowships for Minority Students
  - Predoctoral Fellowships for Students with Disabilities
  - Individual Postdoctoral Fellowships

Federal Grants

This list is not meant to be all-inclusive but represents the more common granting agencies.

National Institutes of Health

The National Institutes of Health (NIH) was begun as a laboratory for hygiene in 1887. It has grown into 25 separate institutes and centers. The mission is to uncover new knowledge for the betterment of health. It is one of eight health agencies under the Public Health Services, a part of the Department of Health and Human Services (DHHS). NIH sets research priorities in each of the institutes and publicizes them on their web site. About 10 percent of the research dollars goes to intramural research programs; the remaining percentage goes toward extramural research. The intramural projects are those conducted within the confines of the NIH campus, and extramural projects can be anywhere in the world. The current institutes and centers are:

- National Cancer Institute
- National Center for Complementary and Alternative Medicine
- National Center for Research Resources
- National Eye Institute
- National Heart, Lung, and Blood Institute
- National Human Genome Research Institute
- National Institute of Diabetes and Digestive and Kidney Diseases
- National Institute on Drug Abuse
- National Institute of Environmental Health Sciences
- National Institute of General Medical Sciences
- National Institute of Mental Health
- National Institute of Neurological Disorders and Stroke
- National Institute of Nursing Research (NINR)
- National Library of Medicine
- National Institute on Alcohol Abuse and Alcoholism
- National Institute of Allergy and Infectious Diseases
- National Institute of Arthritis and Musculoskeletal and Skin Diseases
- National Institute of Child Health and Human Development
- National Institute on Deafness and Other Communication Disorders
- National Institute of Dental and Craniofacial Research
- Center for Information Technology
- Center for Scientific Review
- John E. Fogarty International Center
- Warren Grant Magnuson Clinical Center

NIH funds health professionals and scientists across disciplines. Most grants are competitive and the requests for proposals or applications are widely available through the web site (http://www.nih.gov) or the national library system. The dates or cycles of funding as well as the priorities are listed. The main source of information is through the NIH Guide to Grants and Contracts. The contact person at NIH is included in all postings about grants, and it is this person's job to assist with grant preparation. Use their expertise when preparing your grant. They will guide you in the process of putting a grant together. Remember the contact person is there to help potential grantees submit the best possible grant. All NIH (including NINR, CDC, DHHS, and AHRQ) use similar application processes and the PHS-398 form unless otherwise specified.

National Institute for Nursing Research

The NINR is but one of the NIH institutes. It will be discussed separately because many nurses apply for its grant monies. In 1985, the NINR first was established as a Center for Research. In 1986, the center moved under the auspices of NIH. Finally in 1993 the Center was changed to an Institute, opening a portion of the NIH funds to its services. The structure and function of NINR changed: Becoming an institute gave it an equal status with the other institutes of health. Fund allocations now came from the general NIH budget. This placed nursing research (even though non-nurses can apply) on par with other disciplines at a federal level.

The National Advisory Council for Nursing Research, primarily composed of nurses, provides a second-level review of grants. The council recommends to the Director of NINR which grants should be funded. Each grant that is submitted receives a priority score but only a certain percentage are awarded funding. The grants are judged on scientific merit and the relevance of the proposed project to NINR's funding priorities.

NINR also supports the training of nurse researchers for expanding the cadre of nurse researchers. Thus almost 10 percent of the 1999 budget was focused on pre- and post-doctoral training grants; less than 7 percent was for career development grants and core centers in specialized areas of research; 3 percent were for intramural programs; and the remaining funds were used for extramural research programs. NINR participates in joint research programs with DHHS, Health Related Services Agency (HRSA), Agency for Healthcare Research and Quality (AHRQ), and the CDC.

The current NIH funding priorities are

- Chronic illnesses
- Quality and cost effectiveness of care
- Health promotion and disease prevention
- Management of symptoms
- Adaptation to new technologies
- Health disparities (differences in the health either among age, social, or ethnic groups)
- Palliative care at the end of life

The emphasis in these areas is on clinical research involving direct patient contact or basic science linked directly to patient problems.

The mission of NINR is to establish a scientific basis for health care across the life span. Multidisciplinary or collaborative research remains a thrust of intramural projects. The NINR goals for 2000 to 2004 are to

- Identify and support research opportunities that will achieve scientific distinction and produce significant contributions to health.
- Identify and support future areas of opportunity to advance research on high-quality, cost-effective care and to contribute to the scientific base for nursing practice.
- Communicate and disseminate research findings resulting from NINR-funded research.
- Enhance the development of nurse researchers through training and career development opportunities (NINR 2001).

Centers for Disease Control and Prevention

The CDC is one of eight federal public health agencies. The CDC's mission is to promote health and the quality of life by disease, injury, and disability control and prevention. The CDC includes eleven Centers, Institutes, and offices. They are the

- National Center for Chronic Disease Prevention and Health Promotion
- National Center for Environmental Health
- National Center for Health Statistics
- National Center for HIV, STD, and TB Prevention
- National Center for Infectious Diseases
- National Center for Injury Prevention and Control
- National Immunization Program
- National Institute for Occupational Safety and Health
- Office of Genetics and Disease Prevention
- Office of Global Health
- Public Health Practice Program Office

The CDC funds public health conferences. This agency also forms cooperative agreements (through competitive grants) in the areas of

- AIDS/HIV
- Chronic disease prevention and health promotion
- Diabetes control and disability
- Emerging infections
- Environmental health
- Immunization, injury, and violence prevention and control
- Minority health/health promotion
- Occupational safety and health
- Sexually transmitted diseases
- Tuberculosis

The request for proposals (RFP) and request for applications (RFA) forms are available from their web site (www.cdc.gov) or in the national library system.

The CDC is very active in global health initiatives: Health education in the form of distance-based graduate degree programs in public health in developing countries is another fundable area.

Department of Health and Human Services Training Grants

The DHHS is the largest grant-making agency in the federal government. It contains the

- Administration for Children and Families (ACF)
- Health Care Financing Administration (HCFA)

- Centers for Disease Control and Prevention (CDC)
- Agency for Toxic Substances and Disease Registry (ATSDR)
- Food and Drug Administration (FDA)
- Health Resources and Services Administration (HRSA)
- Indian Health Service (IHS)
- National Institutes of Health (NIH)
- Substance Abuse and Mental Health Services Administration (SAMHSA)

The mission is to enhance the health and well-being of Americans through support of effective health and human services. The DHHS goals focus on improving quality of care through health services and education. One of the core values is to form partnerships among government, universities, and the private sector to improve quality of care. The DHHS challenges that impact on quality of care are

- Managed care transformation
- Rising number of uninsured Americans
- Changes in the composition of the American family
- Aging of America
- Rising costs associated with chronic illness
- Need for collaborative health care partnerships-patients need care coordination among the specialists attending their health needs
- Genetic breakthroughs
- Privacy of health care information
- Emerging and re-emerging infectious diseases
- Changing role of the government in health care (DHHS 2001)

The DHHS administers approximately 300 different grant programs. The Catalog of Federal Domestic Assistance (CFDA) is the official listing of these grants and is available through GrantsNet on line (www.grantsnet.org). *Who's Who in Federal Grants Management* is a quick resource for all federal grant agencies and their management offices.

DHHS provides funding opportunities for educational grants. Some are very specific to a disease entity such as cancer education, whereas others are for basic or advanced education. Beginning in fiscal year 2000, Advanced Education Nursing Traineeship Grants that were previously funded have to reapply. Only one grant application from an institution is recommended for grants that are similar in content. For example, a primary care women's health nurse practitioner grant and a pediatric nurse practitioner training grant from the same institution could be combined to simplify panel review. If the grants, however, are from different areas or there is a compelling need for each grant, then the institution may choose to submit more than one grant during a funding cycle. These changes are part of the Nursing Education and Practice Improvement Act of 1998 (DHHS 2001).

Training grants are well known to most educators. They provide the monies to support nursing programs, especially at the advanced practice level. These grants are part of Title VIII of the Public Health Service Act, programs administered by the HRSA, Bureau of Health Professions, Division of Nursing. The purpose of these grants is to support education with the long-term outcome of improving health care delivery. The funding cycle is generally once or twice per year, but depends on the particular grant. Grants are reviewed on the merits of the curriculum, availability of faculty, faculty expertise and credentials, and media resources, as well as the potential to draw a population of students. The request for proposals or applications can be found along with other federal grants at the HRSA web site (www.hrsa.dhhs.gov/grants.htm).

Examples of these training grants are numerous, and include

- Academic Administrative Units in Primary Care
- Pre-doctoral Training in Primary Care
- Physician Assistants Training in Primary Care
- Residency Training in Primary Care
- Faculty Development in Primary Care
- Podiatric Residency in Primary Care
- Model State Supported Area Health Education Center (AHEC)
- Geriatric Education Centers
- Geriatric Training Regarding Physicians and Dentists
- Allied Health Special Projects, Public Health Training Centers
- Health Administration Traineeships and Special Projects
- Health Careers Opportunity Program
- Centers of Excellence
- Basic Nurse Education and Practice
- Advanced Education Nursing
- Nursing Workforce Diversity
- Advanced Education Nursing Traineeships
- Advanced Education Nursing-Nurse Anesthetist Traineeships
- Public Health Experience in State and Local Health Departments for Baccalaureate Nursing Programs

During this time of a critical nursing shortage, training grants are an important aspect of recruitment and retention of faculty positions. Undergraduate and graduate student enrollments have significantly dropped over the last 5 years. DHHS has funds available to schools that are interested in recruiting minority students and faculty and then retaining them. DHHS places a high priority in getting junior high and high school students excited about a health services career. Thus, a part of the undergraduate or special projects grants contain an element of Kids Into Health Careers, a program aimed at marketing the positive aspects of health careers. Schools should include how they are going to implement this form of recruitment. A major debate has arisen over the past few years about whether the training grant is able to demonstrate retention as well as strong recruitment strategies. Recruitment costs are high and not profitable to the nursing profession if they are not successful in retaining the students.

Training grants at the advanced practice level are more likely to have a community-based focus and some component of distance learning. Some grants have demonstrated the need for a specific specialty program within a geographic area. The institutions, however, may lack the faculty expertise or dollars to support a freestanding program. For example, the University of Kansas, University of Missouri, and Wichita State University formed a consortium program for Neonatal Nurse Practitioners, and the University of Cincinnati College of Nursing and Ohio State University started a joint nurse midwifery program. The latter was funded at the state rather than federal level. But in each of these examples, the partnership meant bringing together competitors to sit at the table and work out a joint curriculum or neither program would be able to start. Are these joint programs difficult? Yes, at times, but it is a successful strategy for receiving federal funds.

Many schools are also recognizing that at the graduate level they cannot be all things to all people; thus, Centers of Excellence are being established. An institution will build a reputation for a certain type of graduate education such as oncology nursing or substance abuse. The center concept provides a strong support component for resources when other grant funds for specific education are sought. Center grants are also available through various governmental agencies. Center grant writing is beyond the scope of this chapter, but it is important to remember that they exist and remain a potential source of funding in certain well-established research academic or health care centers. The Center Training Grant may provide a tangible commitment on the part of the institution to support specific, focused training.

Agency for Healthcare Research and Quality (Formerly the Agency for Health Care Policy and Research)

The AHRQ has gained more recognition over the last 5 years. It was started in 1989 to bridge the gap between biomedical research knowledge and the delivery of health care. The focus of AHRQ research is to find answers to questions about the population served, the costs involved, and what form of delivery system works best (Jones, Tulman, and Clancy 1999). This agency supports both intramural and extramural research. Special emphasis is on minority health care, women's and children's health, international health, ethical issues in health care, and analyses of cost-effectiveness of delivery systems (Jones, Tulman, and Clancy 1999). Extramural research may be grant applications or cooperative agreements and contracts. Requests for proposals or applications are available at the AHRQ web site (http://www.ahrq.gov/fund/98049.htm). The time cycle is included in the information found at this site.

Some grants are only given annually, while others are rolling (submission is not time dependent). Project officers are ready and willing to help the potential grantee write a successful grant. They encourage calls early in the grant writing process.

AHRQ suggests that a three- to seven-page concept paper be submitted first for critique rather than waiting to submit an entire grant. This concept paper is not required (see Appendix D for a sample abbreviated concept paper). Four study sections conduct grant reviews. They are Health Systems Research, Health Care Quality and Effectiveness Research, Health Care Technology and Decision Sciences, and Health Research Dissemination and Implementation (Jones, Tulman, and Clancy 1999).

Grants are reviewed for scientific and technical merit and how well they fit with the priorities of the agency. This agency looks at grants as to their policy relevance or impact on policy making. Use of a multidisciplinary team is favored in research grants. A population or aggregate focus is also suggested. The project officer may contact the principal investigator after the first level review for clarification of certain areas of the grant (Jones, Tulman, and Clancy 1999). This practice is generally not done by other federal agencies. As with the other federal agencies, AHRQ funds R01 (research grants that meet priority areas), R03 (small grants, which are often pilots or dissertation grants), R13 (conference grants), and F32 (individual postdoctoral research training grants) (Jones, Tulman, and Clancy 1999).

Corporate or Small Business Grants

Corporate or small business grants may be awarded by specific corporations or foundations, as well as through the small business grant office at the federal level primarily through the Office of Extramural Research of the NIH. The NIH offers the following grants:

- Small Business Innovation Research (SBIR)
- Small Business Technology Transfer (STTR)

The SBIR program's aim is to support small businesses that have the potential for commercializing research. Biomedical and behavioral research are two of the priority funding areas. The STTR program is a cooperative agreement between a small business and a research institution. Innovation and commercialization of research are two the major criteria for these grants. On the web site (http://www.grants.nih.gov/grants/funding/sbir.htm) there is a link to the previous SBIR and STTR Awards, which provides an abstract of successful grants and contact information on the project directors. This web site also has two links to help small businesses develop. They are the National Venture Capital Association and the National Association of Small Business Investment Companies.

Funding is also available from venture capitalists who are independent contractors or associated with larger parent companies. For the venture capitalist, the return may be a percentage of the business, or they may offer to buy the company if it supports other corporations that they own. The list of potential companies is endless. There are online services such as Liberty Online and Federal Money Retriever that will match a business with a potential financial backer. State Departments of

Commerce are another good resource. For example, the State of Illinois has an initiative to advance Illinois technology. Funds are available to support science and technology projects, university commercialization centers, and technology transfer activities. Other resources are universities themselves; West Texas A&M University, University of Cincinnati, and Indiana University have all supported special projects including small businesses.

Recently, small business grants have emphasized start up monies for women attempting to start their own businesses. These businesses can be for-profit or not-for-profit companies. The grant applications are clear about what will or will not be covered in such grants. Like all other grants the funding priorities are available.

Examples of resources for small business grants beside those listed above include professional organizations and magazines. They include *Entrepreneur Magazine*, National Association for Female Executives, National Association for Women Business Owners, and Service Corps of Retired Executives (SCORE).

Special Projects of Regional and National Significance

Special Projects of Regional and National Significance (SPRANS) grants are special projects or demonstration programs that are funded through the Maternal Child Health Board (MCHB) and other federal agencies such as Health Resources and Services Administration (HRSA). The thrust is to support innovative programs, training, and research in maternal child health. For example, the Cincinnati Center for Developmental Disorders and Children's Hospital Adolescent Clinic identified a need for more training in adolescent health issues for physicians and nurses. The Director of Nursing at the Adolescent Clinic spearheaded the writing of several SPRANS grants to support educational activities. A few of these SPRANS evolved into nursing electives for the University of Cincinnati's undergraduate and graduate students. Traineeships for health professionals that desired training in the area of adolescent health were also made available through SPRANS.

Demonstration projects highlight changes in health care delivery or in the communities' health care needs. The rationale for these programs is to determine the feasibility of providing a service or expanding an educational program such as adolescent health education. If the pilot project is successful, other funding sources or the parent organization such as a university takes over the continuing costs. These projects generally provide strong positive public relations for the institution because they serve a community need. These grants can be a win-win situation. The down side is that when the funding dries up, these programs end, returning a population of patients to having no services again. This situation has happened many times when substance abuse clinics have been started, run well for the funding cycle, and then closed once the funds were gone. Reassurances are supposed to be made to the funding source that programs will continue at least for a time after the project's end, but in these tight financial times that is not always possible.

Another example is Georgetown University's National Center for Education in Maternal Child Health. This program represents a SPRANS Synthesis Project to bring together information and data derived from SPRANS programs across the country. These data are used to support needs for other grants or to change practice services. Healthy Tomorrows Partnership for Children Program (HTPCP) Analysis and Synthesis Project-Georgetown University is an example of a grant that is impacting practice. This project includes support from the American Academy of Pediatrics for the purpose of blending public health resources with professional pediatric expertise. The synthesis aspect of this program includes data from 107 nationwide projects. These are but two examples of special projects. The website http://www.ncemch.org/spr/default.html provides links to other projects.

Conclusion

Many resources exist for funding. Some of these monies are only awarded for research, whereas others are for clearly educational and demonstration projects. The latter grant category helps to support new innovative clinical programs or expansion of existing programs to meet community health care needs. The entrepreneur also has resources within the federal government and private sector to "grow" a small business. Today these small businesses provide services to health care professionals or their patients that otherwise might not be available.

The Grant Process 3

Requests for Applications or Proposals

Grant applications can be solicited from individuals or corporations for specific projects or target audiences. The more common route for grant applications is a call for submission. These are referred to as *request for applications* (RFAs) or *request for proposals* (RFPs). The RFA represents a call for an application for a research, education, or clinical innovation program. The application is to determine the congruency between the project's specific aims and the aims of the funding agency. If the application meets the mission and funding priorities, a request will be made for a full proposal.

An RFP is a call for a complete project plan. Normally, there is no application step in this process. The first submission is the final submission of the grant proposal. The requests for proposals are found in most foundation or federal listservs. The Grantsinfo web site (grantsinfo@nih.gov) is one central location for grants. The individual web site addresses or mailing addresses listed at the back of this book are other places that RFAs or RFPs can be obtained.

The RFA or RFP gives the potential grant writer information about the funding priorities, cycle for funding, amount of funding, ways the monies may be used, contact person, and how to obtain the actual grant application. The RFP may give the specific objectives of the call for grants. Specific aims, target audience, and eligibility criteria for both the grant population and the grant seeker are outlined in the requests. You must adhere to these elements in the application/proposal. If a letter of inquiry or intent (see Appendix D) is necessary before the actual grant is submitted, the RFA or RFP will contain this information. The RFP will also specify the format of the grant application, where to mail the completed application, and how to mail the application. Failure to follow these rules will nullify the grant's review.

Reviewing the RFP is a good way to determine the "hot topics" for funding opportunities. Information about the review process and release of funds is also included in the RFP. The time frame varies among the various funding agencies ranging from a matter of weeks to many months. Some agencies will provide the grant writer opportunities to review similar grants that have been funded in the past. These documents can be helpful when beginning to fill out the RFP. For example, Training or Special Projects grants through the Department of Health and Human Services (DHHS) are available on site for review. If you can make a trip to Washington DC, make an appointment to conduct such a review. You may also want to consider asking one of the past grant awardees to serve as a consultant to your grant. Use of such a consultant strengthens your grant application. After all, the grantee has been successful at receiving funding and is known to the funding agency.

The contact person listed for the grant application is an excellent resource. This person is there to answer specific questions as you are working on the grant. Establishing a relationship with such a person is an invaluable contact if you have never written a grant before. Even the seasoned grant writer can benefit from working with the contact person. After all, the funding agencies want the grants to be sent in good shape and with complete information. Using your resources is not cheating, but wise use of available technical help!

Always keep in mind that the proposal must grab the attention of the reader. Make the grant easy to follow and conform to the basic rules of learning. Tell me, and then tell me again to "sell" the key points. When many grants are being reviewed in a cycle, the more concise, crisp, and clean you make it for the grant reader the more likely small flaws will be forgiven. The proposal is a marketing tool. You are selling your institution, yourself, and your research team to the buyer—the funding agency. Now let's see how that is done.

Research Grants

Three basic characteristics comprise a dynamite research proposal. The first characteristic is a *meaningful question.* Meaningful to you is not always important to the funding agency. Again, this is where congruency of your project to the funding agency's mission and goals is critical. This characteristic was addressed in Chapter 1. The second characteristic of a strong proposal is ensuring that the proposal represents *good science.* Good science requires thorough planning and knowing the state of the science in the proposed area of study. Chapter 1 provided a few recommendations for how the grantee might stay abreast of the science. The final characteristic of a dynamite proposal is that of *careful application techniques* in writing the proposal. The grantee must ensure that the proposal complies with all instructions and should take the same care that a writer does when submitting a scientific publication. The writing style should be clear and lucid, free of grammatical and typographical errors. The proposal should be neat and all the major components and supportive documents should be arranged in a logical order.

Clarity and consistency within the grant is one of the major challenges that a grant writer must address. Constructing a research grant application is much like using building blocks: The specific aims form the foundation and structure for the research proposal. From the specific aims, the research design and methods are chosen to answer the identified research questions and hypotheses. The research design and aims are then used to formulate appropriate statistical analyses. One of the ways to promote clarity between hypotheses, variables, instruments, and data analyses is to organize the research proposal by key study variables contained within the specific aims and research questions and hypotheses. For example, consistently use special font styles such as bolding or italics to highlight these variables throughout the sections of the grant. (See the research plan in Appendix D.) But make sure that these formatting options are allowable by the funding agency. Determine this by the guidelines given to you by the funding agency. Also addressing the variables in a consistent order throughout the sections of the proposal may also promote clarity and consistency. Finally, well-designed tables and figures can greatly enhance the presentation of materials related to research design and methods.

The major components of a research grant application include the (a) abstract, (b) research plan, (c) references, (d) budget, (e) curriculum vitae or biosketch, (f) other support, (g) resources, (h) institutional review board approvals, and (i) appendices. (See Appendix D for a sample Face Sheet.) Although the research grant has been used as the exemplar for this chapter, all elements described here are generally the same with any grant application such as training and special projects, which are discussed later in this chapter. Instead of a research plan, other grants may use the terminology "plan and implementation" or "methodology." The individual sections of a research grant will be discussed below.

Abstract

Proposals often begin with a short summary of the proposed research. The abstract is usually written last and summarizes the specific aims, background and significance, and research design and methods sections. The greatest challenge to writing this section is adhering to the word limit. An editor can be extremely useful by helping you cut out unnecessary words and phrases. Remember, too, the abstract sets the stage for the remainder of the proposal. Make sure that if it is written early in the grant writing process, any changes that are made in the body of the grant are reflected in the abstract. Take great pains in writing the abstract because if it is flawed and it is the first thing the reader sees of your scholarship, it can set the grant up for a more critical review. Paying attention to details especially in the abstract to catch the reader's attention is of the utmost importance in "selling" the grant's idea (see the sample abstract in Appendix D).

Research Plan

The research plan is the most critical component of the proposal. The research plan should be clear, concise, and cogent while at the same time containing sufficient information to evaluate the proposal. Although some research plans allow the grantee to include appendices, it cannot be assumed that all reviewers will receive the appendices in the review process. Therefore, the research plan must contain all critical information needed to evaluate the quality of the proposal, independent of any other document. Longer is not better in the case of grant applications or research plans; concise yet detailed plans should be the aim. Although the format for the research plan may vary depending on the funding source, most research plans include the following sections: specific aims; background and significance; preliminary studies; design and methods, and references (see Appendix D).

Specific Aims

The section on specific aims of the study describes the purpose(s) of the study, what the research intends to accomplish, and the long-term goals or potential usefulness of the educational or research program. Although the organization of this section may vary, most researchers start with the purpose(s) of the study. The statement of purpose usually includes the key study variables and their possible interrelationships, and the nature of the population of interest (Polit and Hungler 1998). For example,

> The purpose of this research is to assess the relationship between three sets of variables: (a) light and sound levels in the neonatal intensive care unit (NICU), (b) sleep and wake patterns of preterm infants, and (c) physiologic and behavioral responses of preterm infants to a painful stimulus—a heel stick for necessary blood sampling (Walden 2000).

Another example is for a grant on Perinatal Alcohol Users: Identification and Intervention. The specific aims of this study were to:

> (1) identify alcohol users/abusers at risk for delivering an infant with Fetal Alcohol Syndrome/Fetal Alcohol Effects; (2) educate pregnant woman's health professionals regarding the identification of and the adverse effects of alcohol on the woman and her offspring, and (3) evaluate the effectiveness of interventions by comparing this group of mothers and infants to those randomly selected as a control group to those followed in the Perinatal, Newborn Division, and Child and Family Health Services Pediatric Tracking databases (Kenner 1991).

Following the statement of purpose, the grantee can include a description of the problem that the research intends to solve or help solve. For example,

Pain research in neonates has focused primarily on behavioral and physiologic responses to brief clinical procedures in healthy, full-term infants, and in older, physiologically stable preterm infants. None have investigated the relationship of infant sleep patterns and light and noise levels in the NICU, to infant responses to pain. Knowledge of these factors may help caregivers to promote a healing micro-environment within the NICU that may help infants to cope with painful clinical procedures and minimize the long-term neurobehavioral consequences of chronic pain in the NICU (Walden 2000).

For the Perinatal Alcohol Users grant, the significance section started with:

"Although the amount of research related to Fetal Alcohol Syndrome (FAS)/ Fetal Alcohol Effects (FAE) is increasing, little published research is available concerning strategies to improve health providers identification of and interventions with alcohol using/abusing pregnant women. Current literature tends to be opinion based and exhorts the reader to be more aware of and prepared to intervene with these women. These authors seem to agree that health care professionals are not effectively identifying women at risk for or currently using/abusing alcohol. If they are identified, interventions are seldom implemented. When health care providers select an intervention it must be made intuitively because few studies are in the literature demonstrating the effectiveness of different intervention strategies.

Interventions are needed to increase the identification of women at risk for delivering a FAS/FAE infant. Once identified by health care professionals, a referral can be made to a case manager who can then enroll and maintain the woman in prenatal care" (Kenner 1991).

Many proposals will include a conceptual framework that helps the researcher to organize the study and interpret the research findings. The conceptual framework clarifies concepts and the proposed relationships among the concepts in a study. The concepts of the study can then be stated in the form of a research question (for exploratory or descriptive research) or more commonly as a research hypothesis. Research questions are often used when knowledge is insufficient to formulate a hypothesis. An example of a research question is:

Do light (as measured by a light meter), noise (as measured by a dosimeter), and sleep/wake state patterns (as measured by Als State Scale) in the 2 hours before a heel stick procedure explain the preterm neonate's physiological and behavioral responses to a heel stick procedure as measured by the Premature Infant Pain Profile (PIPP)? (Walden 2000).

A directional hypothesis based on the above research question might read,

> Preterm neonates cared for in environments that have higher light (as measured by a light meter) and noise (as measured by a dosimeter) levels in the 2 hours preceding a heel stick procedure will demonstrate fewer physiological and behavioral responses to a heel stick procedure (as measured by the PIPP).

Another example is given in the concept paper in Appendix D. This letter concerns use of Dame Saunders' conceptual model of "Whole Person Suffering." If a study is undertaken using this model, then the concepts of the model form the foundation for the research questions and guide the data collection. In this example, the concepts are physical, psychologic, spiritual, and social. The emphasis in this model is on maximizing quality of life and function, not the medical model of cure. If the proposed study is a randomized clinical control trial, the interventions would involve maximizing quality of life and function in a specific population.

The specific aims section usually concludes with a brief discussion of the long-term goal or potential usefulness of the research. For example,

> The long-term aims of this program of research are to investigate nursing interventions that promote a restful environment and optimal sleep patterns for high-risk neonates, and consequently, alter the establishment of the chronic pain response and long-term consequences of pain in preterm neonates. (Walden 2000).

In summary, the specific aims should be clear, well developed, logical, attainable, and distinct (Fuller, Hasselmeyer, Hunter, Abdellah, and Hinshaw 1991). The goals of the research proposal should be of major significance in terms of the health of the people of the United States of America. A well-written specific aims section is crucial and should guide the research design and methods.

Background and Significance

This section discusses not only what is currently known to be related to the proposed area of study, but also more importantly, the significance of the research. It is important to convince the readers that this study is the next logical step based on the state of the science. It is also important to show how this research addresses a widespread or significant health concern. Linking your proposed research to national health objectives such as *Healthy People 2010* (see Appendix C for *Healthy People 2010* objectives) or federal or professional organizational research priorities (see Appendix D for examples) will strengthen the likelihood of funding for the proposed research.

The literature review ties together the concepts put forth in the conceptual framework. For example in the Whole Person Suffering Model, each of the four areas (physical, psychological, spiritual, and social) should be covered in the review of literature. In addition, the phenomenon of interest (e.g., pain) would have a review section. Today, with the emphasis on evidence-based practice, the thrust is to use integrated reviews on specific topics to support a proposed area of study, intervention, or educational program. Systematic or integrated reviews are available on the Internet. Databases such as the Cochrane Collaborative, Vermont Oxford Database, or specific topic reviews like The Joanna Briggs Institute for Evidence Based Nursing and Midwifery are available. These databases house findings and reviews of different levels of research, but primarily contain randomized clinical control trials. The information available from these integrated reviews provides a strong foundation for your study's question, research plan, and background and significance sections of your grant application.

The literature reviewed to support your proposal should be both relevant and current. Move beyond simply summarizing the literature to critically evaluating existing knowledge and identifying gaps in the scientific evidence. If a conceptual framework is used, it should be clearly tied to the present study, but also well mapped to other parts of the application. A conceptual framework is a visual way of demonstrating relationships that are known and ones that have not been investigated and may be the focus of your study. Finally, the background should clearly support the specific aims of the study.

Preliminary Studies

Although some grants do not require preliminary studies for a competitive edge for research funding, all grants depend, to a certain extent, on the principal investigator's ability to convince the reviewers of their competence to carry out the proposed research. Research competence is most often determined by experience in the proposed area of study, a proven research track record, and scholarly publications (Tournquist and Funk 1990).

In addition to demonstrating the competence of the principal investigator, preliminary studies also help to demonstrate the feasibility of the methods being proposed. The pilot research should be described in detail, including the hypotheses/research questions, methods, and study findings. The principal investigator should demonstrate how the preliminary studies or pilot data have led to the current proposed study.

If no preliminary or pilot studies have been conducted, the grant writer should use other professional accomplishments to demonstrate clinical expertise and leadership in the proposed area of study. Publications or presentations in the proposed area of study demonstrate clinical expertise in the study topic. Copies of relevant publications make a nice addition to the grant in the appendices, if allowed. A brief summary of the expertise and productivity of the research team highlights the team's skill. Thread this expertise throughout the biosketches to show further clinical and research expertise.

Research Design and Methods

The research design is the strategic plan that the researcher uses to accomplish the specific aims and answer or test the research questions and hypotheses. Most research designs can be categorized as either quantitative or qualitative. *Quantitative research* focuses on counting or quantifying data. The research questions answered by this method are concerned with finding relationships, causality between variables, and predicting outcomes. The major classifications of quantitative research are descriptive or observational, case, time sequenced or longitudinal, prospective, historical, and experimental studies (Moody 1990). The gold standard for experimental studies remains the randomized clinical control trials (RCTs), but there are also quasi-experimental designs used as many clinical studies cannot control all the variables necessary to make it a randomized controlled trial.

Qualitative research describes "what is" according the person or phenomenon being studied. The six characteristics of qualitative research are "a belief in multiple realities, a commitment to identifying an approach to understanding that will support the phenomenon studied, commitment to the participant's point of view, conduct of inquiry in a way that does not disturb the natural context of the phenomena of interest, acknowledged participation of the researcher in the research, and conveyance of the understanding of the phenomena by reporting in a literary style rich with participant's commentary" (Streubert and Carpenter, 1995, p. 10). Different forms of qualitative research include descriptive, phenomenological, and ethnographic studies. Within these methods there are specific approaches such as grounded theory and historical methods. There are too many to list, but each approach follows the characteristics of qualitative studies.

It is beyond the scope of this reference to provide detailed descriptions of both design methodologies; suffice it to say that the best design for your study is the design that flows logically from the problem statement, literature review, theoretical framework, and research question or hypothesis. The choice of a research design is a major research decision. Therefore, the strongest research design feasible should be used to maximize the credibility and dependability of the study findings. For a comparison of quantitative and qualitative research methods please see Table 3-1.

Examples of a qualitative and quantitative research question come from my "Transition to Home" work. For my first study I wanted to find out, "What it was like for a mother taking a baby home from a neonatal unit?" "What concerns or problems the mothers had during the first and fourth weeks at home with the baby?" and finally "What could we have done differently at the hospital to ease the transition to home?" I used a phenomenological approach to this research. I repeated this qualitative study in three different settings. From these data I developed a "Transition Questionnaire" based on the five categories of concern that evolved from the qualitative studies. The Transition Questionnaire was a quantifiable tool used to measure the phenomenon of transition. While I was still concerned with the three original research questions, I now used the Transition Questionnaire to measure the mothers' responses. The questionnaire quantified their answers.

Once the research design is chosen, the researcher should clearly describe the design and methods as well as the rationale for selection. The researcher should articu-

TABLE 3-1 Comparison of Qualitative and Quantitative Research Methods

Quantitative	Qualitative
Objective	Subjective value
One reality	Multiple realities
Reduction, control, prediction	Discovery, description, understanding
Measurable	Interpretive
Mechanistic	Organismic
Parts equal the whole	Whole is greater than the parts
Report statistical analyses	Report rich narrative
Researcher separate	Researcher part of research process
Subjects	Participants
Context free	Context dependent

Streubert and Carpenter 1995. Reproduced by permission of Lippincott, Wiliams & Wilkins.

late other designs that were considered and the rationale for why the proposed research design is superior to the alternate designs. For example, clinical researchers often choose a quasi-experimental design over a stronger true experimental design because of the inability to physically or ethically manipulate certain variables. These variables include such elements as overall neonatal intensive care lighting, the heating level within an incubator, or withholding of true pain medication and giving a placebo for an adult with cancer.

Clearly state the assumptions and limitations of the proposed research. If problems are anticipated, possible solutions or strategies should be discussed to minimize their occurrence. For example, in longitudinal studies, subject attrition is expected and the principal investigator should include a discussion of strategies to maintain subject participation over time.

Six basic elements comprise the research design: setting and sample; description of intervention, if applicable; instruments, data collection procedures; data analyses; and timeline. These elements are briefly discussed below.

Setting and Sample. Provide a description of the setting chosen for the study along with the rationale for its selection. Describe in detail the type of setting, location, and typical patient population. State specifically why this particular setting was chosen over other possible settings. Furthermore, if you select a distant site over a local site, it is important that you provide a rationale for that decision. Address how distance will affect data collection and quality of data collection methods. For instance, the grant writer may describe a plan for the selection of a site coordinator employed by the clinical agency or one who lives in close proximity of the site as a strategy to handle the issue of distance. The proposal must also address plans for ensuring appropriate training and reliability of research assistants, and plans to monitor the site to ensure the integrity of data collection methods. Finally, the researcher must document that the research site is willing to provide the researcher with access to subjects. This is usually best accomplished by submitting letters of support from key personnel at the study site such as the medical director, nursing director, or other applicable administrative personnel.

Clearly describe the criteria for inclusion and exclusion of subjects in the study. (see the research plan in Appendix D). Depending on the space available in the grant application, the grant writer may want to describe more fully why these criteria were selected and how they help control for threats to external validity. In addition, the researcher has an obligation to convince the reviewer of the adequacy of the site to produce a sufficient number of subjects based on inclusion and exclusion criteria. To address this issue, include in narrative text or table format the number of subjects available per month or year for study at the data collection site who meet the inclusion criteria. In addition to the number of subjects, federal grants often require that the principal investigator address the recruitment of special populations, including gender and racial/ethnic groups as well as women and children. For example, the plan for the recruitment of subjects might read as follows (Walden 2000):

> In 1999, the racial composition of neonatal patients for the respective age groups at the Children's Hospital is 22 percent African American; 29 percent Hispanic; 47 percent Caucasian; and 2 percent Other. The sample composition for this study is expected to be similar. Since the sample population is approximately evenly divided among minority versus non-minority groups, if more than one infant is available for inclusion in the study on any given laboratory collection day, preference will be given to infants of the youngest gestational age. If more than one infant meets the youngest gestational age criteria, preference will be given to recruitment of minority background. The rationale for choosing the youngest subjects as first preference is that there is a smaller pool of infants between 25 to 27 weeks gestational age than 34 to 36 weeks gestational age, making it more difficult to recruit this age sample. The rationale for recruiting minorities is to ensure adequate minority representation, since there will be equipment limitations. The recruitment goal for minority representation is that at least 50 percent of the sample will have a minority background. This percentage represents the actual minority representation at the Children's Hospital. Recruitment will be reviewed monthly regarding minority inclusion.

The sample size of the proposed study is also important to discuss. A power analysis should be performed to justify the proposed sample size. A power analysis calculates the probability that a significant finding will occur. The power is set a priori (before beginning the study). This calculation accounts for the effect size—the number that it will take to achieve support or reject a null hypothesis. The other parameters of the power analysis are the significance criterion ($p < .05$) to be examined and the sample size.

After setting the power at a specified a priori level, the effect size, and the significance level, the fourth parameter is calculated. This process determines the sample size necessary to achieve the power and effect size noted by the researcher prior to conducting the actual study. A power calculation can sometimes put fear into the hearts of novice researchers. There are web- and computer-based programs now available to help with sample size calculation. Base the sample size on the most conservative number needed to answer the research question or hypothesis being proposed. For example, if both hierarchical regression and repeated measures ANOVA statistical analyses are being proposed, use the most conservative sample size numbers that result from running power analyses for each of the different analyses. The researcher should also discuss how sample size is adjusted to account for subject attrition. For example in a previous pilot study, if 15 percent attrition was noted due to mortality of subjects, the sampling plan is adjusted to oversample by 15 percent.

Methods for selecting the sample and assigning subjects to groups, if applicable, should also be discussed. Two basic sampling techniques used in nursing research are probability (random) sampling and nonprobability (nonrandom) sampling. Random sampling techniques are preferred and result in more representative samples; nonprobability sampling techniques are more feasible, practical, and economical. Although random sampling is difficult to achieve in clinical settings, random assignment to groups is often easily accomplished. Subjects can be randomly assigned to treatment conditions by using such methods as flipping a coin, pulling slips from a hat, or more commonly, a table of random digits.

Intervention. If an intervention study is proposed, the grant proposal should clearly describe the intervention protocol. Describe the intervention administration in detail. Include how the treatment condition differs from the control or comparison group. Ideally for larger grants, pilot testing of the intervention is done prior to submission of the grant. However, some granting agencies accept proposals involving pilot work. Once the pilot is completed, the data form the foundation for larger, more competitive grants. If the research proposal does not involve an intervention protocol, omit this section.

An example of an intervention is use of the Brief Intervention Model (BIM). The BIM consists of a 10-minute interview with a person who consumes alcohol. The researcher and the pregnant woman (in the Perinatal Alcohol Users study) set a mutual goal for cutting down on her drinking. At each encounter with the woman the researcher used the BIM to ascertain her drinking and to intervene when and if she had increased or restarted her drinking. Another example of an intervention was the use of a home visit to follow mothers and babies after discharge from a neonatal unit. In describing the home visit intervention, it was important to describe in detail who was responsible for doing the home visit, when they were done, how long they lasted, and specific interventions that were performed at each visit.

Instruments. This section describes each of the study variables and their measurement. The researcher should provide operational definitions for each of the independent and dependent variables within the proposed study. Study variables can also be clarified in a table format that matches each of the independent and dependent variables to a particular instrument or subscale on an instrument. Describe the population, method of administration, reliability, and validity for each instrument used. If alternate instruments are available, the researcher will need to discuss the rationale for the selection of a particular instrument. A sample rationale for pain follows (Walden 2000):

> Pain research has produced several valid and reliable pain instruments, including the CRIES (Krechel and Bildner 1995) and The Premature Infant Pain Profile (Stevens et al. 1996). While the CRIES has been validated for use in infants greater than 32 weeks gestational age, the PIPP can be used in preterm infants below 28 weeks gestational age. Furthermore, the PIPP is preferred over the CRIES in this study as it controls for two significant contextual factors (gestational age and behavioral state) known to modify pain expression in preterm neonates (Craig et al. 1993; Grunau and Craig 1987; Johnston et al. 1993; Stevens and Johnston 1994; Stevens, Johnston, and Horton 1994; Stevens et al. 1993; Johnston et al. 1999). The PIPP will be used to measure acute pain response in this study.

Describe any necessary training of research personnel in the use of each instrument. The researcher should report pilot data or if any is planned for new instruments. Finally, include copies of all instruments in an appendix.

Data Collection Procedures. The description of study procedures usually begins with a clear description of how potential subjects are identified and recruited as participants into the study. This is often followed by a clear description of how and when the intervention will be carried out. Provide the method of data collection. Include aspects of how, when, where, and who uses the instruments. If other study personnel are involved in data collection, a description of their training should be included. Describe the methods used to ensure inter-rater reliability. The researcher should take care to address any potential problems that may be encountered during the study protocol and include the plan for how the problems will be addressed. If the study is complex, a step-by-step procedural checklist should be developed and used by data collectors to ensure that no procedural item is omitted during the course of the study (see the protocol worksheet in Appendix D). If a checklist is used to simplify data collection procedures, include this checklist as an appendix for the reviewers to examine.

Finally, use diagrams of the data collection procedure to clarify the study design and timing of data collection for study instruments. For example, the diagram below was used to illustrate the data collection procedures for the variables contained in the pain study (Walden 2000):

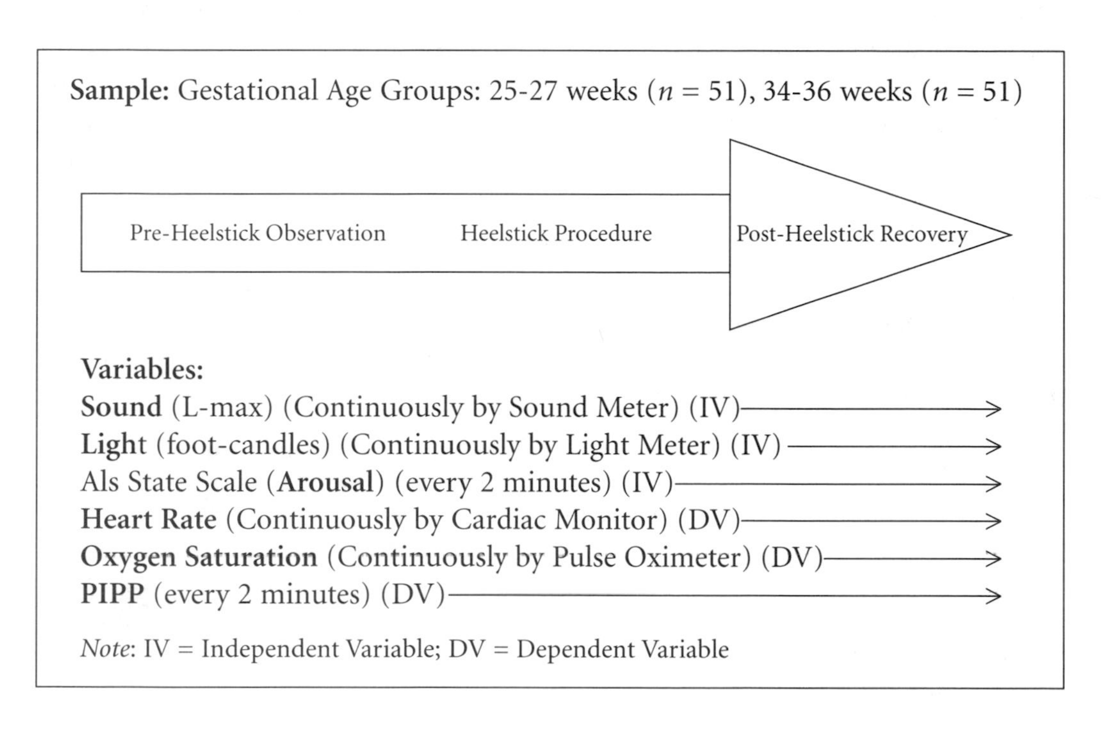

Data Analyses. This section should provide a clear description of plans for data management, refinement, and reduction. Proposals often adequately address the plans for statistical analyses, but fail to provide sufficient detail on how large complex data sets will be reduced for analyses. The researcher should therefore take great care to describe how data will be collated, coded, keyed, and verified.

Base the selection of the statistical analyses on the level and type of data. Furthermore, the statistical analyses should match the specific aims and research questions or hypotheses. Organizing the presentation of data in this section by specific research question or hypothesis is often helpful for both the grant writer and reviewer. The principal investigator may want to consider including a biostatitician on the research team. Involve the statistician early to assist with the development of the statistical plan of the study, including design, analyses, and plan for dissemination of project findings. Often, the biostatistician has the best knowledge and expertise to write this section of the proposal (see the Sample Research Plan for examples of data analyses).

Timeline. The timeline is used to provide an anticipated time frame for project activities including start-up activities such as hiring and training of project personnel, identification of subjects, data collection, data preparation and analysis, and report writing. Be realistic in your time frame; projects always take longer than you expect. It is better to project a longer period of time for a certain aspect of the grant, say the hiring of personnel, so that you will have some slack when other aspects of the grant take longer than expected. This information can be provided in narrative form or the grant writer may chose to present this section in the form of a GANTT Chart, a graph of time relationships. An example of such a GANTT chart from a National Institues of Health (NIH) Area Grant Application is shown in the table below (Walden 2000).

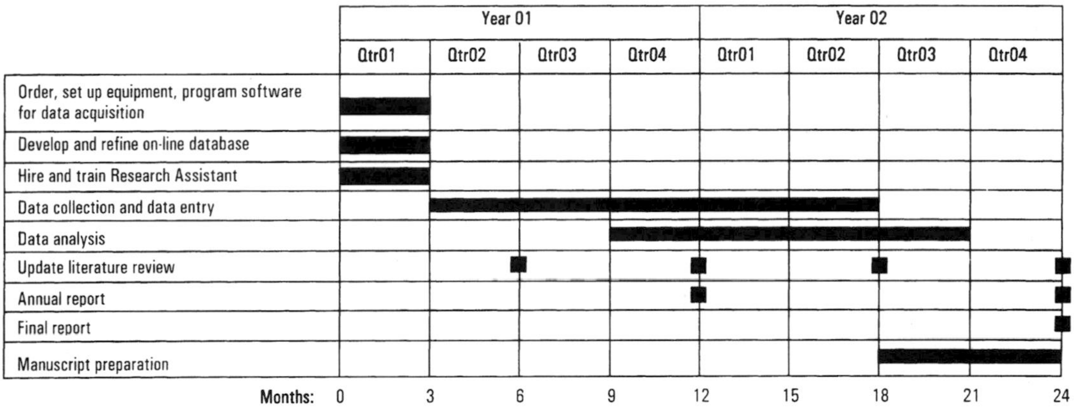

	Year 01				Year 02			
	Qtr01	Qtr02	Qtr03	Qtr04	Qtr01	Qtr02	Qtr03	Qtr04
Order, set up equipment, program software for data acquisition								
Develop and refine on-line database								
Hire and train Research Assistant								
Data collection and data entry								
Data analysis								
Update literature review								
Annual report								
Final report								
Manuscript preparation								

Months: 0 3 6 9 12 15 18 21 24

References

The references section is the last part of your research plan and contains references to journal articles, books, and other materials that you have cited in your grant proposal. Complete bibliographic information should be provided using a consistent referencing format such as the American Psychological Association (APA) style.

Budget

The first important task in creating a budget for the proposal is to review the funding agency's budget criteria closely. The funding agency usually specifies what expenses are allowable and what is not fundable. For example, some grants will not allow for the salary of the principal investigator, but will allow salary dollars allocated for consultants and research assistants. Some federal grants do not allow for travel costs related to dissemination, while others may. Therefore, have a clear idea about the funding guidelines before you start to develop your budget for the proposal.

If you are in an academic center, there may be a research offices with personnel specifically trained to assist you in preparing the budget. The highly experienced staff in these offices can help you obtain salary information, benefit costs, cost of common budget items such as equipment, computers, pagers, mileage, and other costs. Salaries often comprise the largest budget item. For each person listed on the grant, indicate the percentage of commitment to the grant, salary, and fringe benefits. The budget office will assist you in computing indirect costs and setting up subcontracts with other institutions.

Clearly match budget items to grant activities (research personnel, consultants, equipment, supplies, travel, computer costs, and other related expenses). The goal is to ask for what you need to conduct the study. Most funding agencies will request a budget justification for grant expenses. Budget justification is a description of the budget items requested and a rationale for why this expense is needed. Appropriate budget planning will help you to budget appropriately while avoiding the need to pad the budget. Although money can often shift within the same category of the budget, often the budget will not allow shifting of monies between categories such as salary dollars and equipment costs. Therefore, carefully consider where the monies are allocated within the budget.

Federal agencies often use a modular budget process for grant applications requesting up to $250,000 in direct costs per year. For these applications, total direct costs for the proposed study typically are divided into modules of $25,000. Although a standard modular grant application will request the same number of modules in each year of the grant, additional narrative budget justification provides a mechanism for researchers to request variation in the number of modules requested. For example, if the grant involves the purchase of expensive physiologic data acquisition equipment, the principal investigator may want to provide additional budget narrative to explain an increase number of modules for the first year of the grant.

Finally, remember to update the budget as revisions are made throughout the grant writing process to ensure the consistency of the proposal to funding requested. For example, if the sample size changes and thus the amount of time needed to pay a research assistant changes, adjust the budget to reflect these changes (see Appendix D).

Curriculum Vitae or Biosketch

Most funding agencies will ask for professional background for key project personnel such as education, professional experience, research, publications, and honors. Although some agencies may want an abbreviated curriculum vitae, federal agencies commonly ask for a biosketch for project personnel and consultants. Be sure to check the guidelines; most agencies restrict the biosketch to two or three pages. Commonly included on the curriculum vitae or biosketch is a listing of all publications from the past 3 years and any additional references specifically related to the topical area of proposed study. Membership in professional organizations or involvement in community service is usually omitted unless it helps to demonstrate your clinical expertise or leadership ability to carry out the proposed area of study (see Appendix D).

Consultants

One of the hallmarks of a good grant proposal is a capable research team. An aspect that reviewers are asked to evaluate is whether the principal investigator and key project personnel are appropriately trained and suited to carry out the proposed study. Although previous research and publications may help to demonstrate the expertise of the research team, consultants can be used to contribute expertise to the project and enhance the overall quality of the proposal. For example, if an infant researcher's expertise is in pain and the proposal is to examine the interface between pain and sleep, adding a consultant with national recognition in infant sleep may strengthen the credibility of the project and enhance its ability to successfully compete for funding. Another example is a study concerning cancer rehabilitation and exercise physiology. For this study consultants who are expert oncologists coupled with ones who are exercise physiologists are good additions to an academic center grant where no such expertise is on site. Consultants can contribute to the project in a variety of ways, including conceptualization of the study design, selection of research instruments, implementation issues, and data analysis and interpretation.

List names and organizational affiliations for all consultants to the proposed research project. Include a biosketch or curriculum vitae. Although consultant costs may vary, provide a detailed description of the consultation services to be rendered, number of days anticipated for consultation, the expected rate of compensation, and travel, per diem, and other related costs.

Other Support

For federal applications, the funding agency requires information related to active or pending research support for all key project personnel. Other support includes such monetary support as research grants, cooperative agreements, contracts, and institutional awards that project personnel are receiving. Most applications solicit information about the agency providing the support, the project number, if applicable, major goals, dates of approved/proposed project, annual direct costs, percent effort, and any overlap or duplication of efforts between grants. This information allows the granting agency to evaluate the extent to which the funding requested for the proposed research might overlap with other funding sources. This information is also used to ensure that the total sum of time commitments of key project personnel does not individually exceed a 100 percent effort.

Resources

This section should provide a clear description of resources available to conduct the proposed research, primarily, access to availability of adequate resources and accessibility to you of those resources. Depending on the proposed study, this might include a description of available clinical sites, laboratory facilities, office and equipment storage space, library resources, and computer facilities. Letters of support from the agencies involved are often used to validate that the agency has reviewed the study protocol and agrees to allow the principal investigator access to the site and resources needed to conduct the proposed research. (See Appendix D for a sample grant checklist.)

Institutional Review Board Approvals

An Institutional Review Board (IRB) is a panel of health professionals across disciplines and at least one or two consumers. This panel is charged with reviewing any protocol that will be part of a research study. The IRB must ensure scientific merit and protection of human subjects. The IRB must question whether or not a study is ethical or not in relationship to protection of human subjects. For example, many years ago prisoners were used in studies to determine how infectious diseases progressed. These studies were later deemed unethical because a captive population was used. They were probably coerced into participating and they were not informed of potential life-threatening dangers. Today this study could not be done with an IRB sanction. The IRB exists strictly to protect a person's rights and safety in any research study. You cannot conduct a funded project without IRB approval, and in most institutions cannot get any studies done even with staff without IRB approval. The IRB reviews informed consent statements. These statements must be low-level reading (ideally third grade, but no higher than fifth or sixth grade), understandable to the population being tested, and in most instances translated into the population's native language. Protection of human subjects and disclosure of the intervention are important aspects of this process.

This grant section should provide a clear description of procedures for protecting subjects' rights and obtaining informed consent. Discuss measures to protect anonymity or confidentiality related to data collection, management, and storage. Identify potential risks and anticipated benefits of the study. Fully describe potential risks, measures to minimize those risks, and institutional resources available to treat clients who develop health-related complications that arise as a result of the study. Indicate whether the IRB approval process is complete or pending.

If a federal grant is being submitted, the NIH has recently changed its policy in regard to IRB review of research involving human subjects. Previously, NIH required that grant applications have IRB approval at the time of submission or within 60 days after application receipt date. Because fewer than half of all applications submitted to NIH are funded, the NIH has modified its policy to reduce the burden on applicants and IRBs. Beginning with applications submitted on June 1, 2000, IRB approval is not required prior to NIH peer review of an application. However, no grant award can be made without IRB approval. Therefore, following NIH peer review and notification of priority score/percentile, institutions should proceed with IRB review for those applications that have not yet received IRB approval and that appear to be in a fundable range. Applications that involve research with animals will, however, continue to require review by the Institutional Animal Care and Use Committee at the time of submission or within 60 days thereafter.

Appendices

Appendices supplement key information contained within the research plan. Depending on the funding agency, not all reviewers receive the appendices. Ensure that both the abstract as well as the research plan include all pertinent information by which the scientific quality of the proposed study is to be evaluated. That said, the appropriate use of appendices could greatly enhance the research proposal submitted for review. For example, appendices may allow the researcher to provide examples of scholarly writings that help to exemplify the investigators' previous relevant work or to include data collection instruments. Other items commonly included in the appendices are letters of support from consultants and clinical agencies, and subject consent forms.

Revised Applications

If the grant application is resubmitted to the same funding agency and was revised to accommodate suggested revisions from the funding agency, it is important to clearly demonstrate the changes that were made in the grant and to provide answers for any questions the reviewers may have posed. Federal applications usually provide a section prior to the research plan for the principal investigator to address these suggested revisions. When addressing the reviewers' recommendations, all comments are addressed in a collegial fashion. Changes that are made throughout the text can often be italicized to assist the reviewers in identifying the changes that were made in the current application based on previous missing information or recommendations. Finally, remember to update the review of literature and biosketches of study personnel in the current grant application.

Dissemination of Findings

Dissemination of findings is the final outcome of a funded research study. Nursing scholarship cannot advance without dissemination of findings from scientific research. Develop a dissemination plan for all aspects of your scholarship. As you begin to develop a program of research, opportunities exist for dissemination at various levels including publication of literature reviews, theory development, pilot data, instrument development, primary and secondary research questions, serendipitous findings, and secondary analyses. A successful track record of dissemination can only occur if you make this aspect of your scholarship a priority. For most individuals, this means setting aside several hours a day or perhaps one day a week, depending on your schedule and writing style. Because writing can often take second place in a busy academic schedule, it is important to outline your publications and set timelines for submission to keep yourself on track.

Dissemination can take the form of an abstract/poster presentation or written publication. Podium or poster presentations are ideal for dissemination of findings while awaiting publication in a selected scholarly journal. They should not, however, take the place of a scientific publication. If numerous abstract and poster presentations are limiting your manuscript submissions, you may want to consider limiting your speaking engagements to only the scientific presentations that facilitate your career goals. Although it is true that poster or abstract presentations often act as the springboard for manuscript submissions, written dissemination of your data has the potential to contribute more to the scholarship of practice, teaching, and research resulting from a broader and more permanent avenue of dissemination.

When writing for publication, target your journal carefully, based on the objectives you are trying to achieve. If the manuscript's goal is to reach clinicians in a timely manner, you may want to choose a clinical journal with a short publication schedule. If however, the data are not as time sensitive and the goal is to reach a broader audience, you may choose to submit your manuscript to a well-recognized, scholarly journal that has a larger subscription base, but where the timeline for publication following acceptance is longer. In choosing journals, consider nursing as well as non-nursing, discipline-specific journals if the topic is of interest to professionals outside of nursing.

Although rejection of a manuscript by a journal editor is difficult, take the comments provided and use them to improve the manuscript. Ultimately you may choose to resubmit to the same journal or even a different journal after careful evaluation of the journal's target audience. Ideally, when submitting a manuscript, have both a primary and secondary journal in mind. This method will facilitate the resubmission process. To increase your manuscript acceptance rate, you may want to consider setting up a process for scientific review of your manuscripts prior to submission. Select the reviewers based on the type of feedback you are seeking for your manuscript (e.g., copy editing, design and methods, or clinical implications).

Finally, you need to evaluate your dissemination plan periodically and adjust it as necessary. This evaluation should include your publication submission to acceptance ratio. You might find that you need to reorganize your scholarship priorities to increase your publication output. Perhaps you need to develop more realistic goals and timelines for publications.

Dissemination of your finding is exciting. The write up allows you to share your information and build a niche for yourself as you build a professional career. The writing and dissemination through presentations becomes your legacy to the profession and to your family.

Training and Special Projects Grants

Training Grants

Thus far, this chapter has focused on research grants. Training grants essentially follow the same pattern, and contain most of the same elements. An abstract is required that states the problem and its significance, specific aims, and outlines what the training will involve (the educational plan). Instead of focusing on answering a research question, the specific aims require fulfilling educational objectives.

Training grants must include a background and significance section that includes local, state, regional, and national data on potential student population, competing programs, community needs, and resources available to project. For example, I co-wrote a nurse midwifery grant to start a program in southwestern Ohio. There was one program 250 miles north and 150 miles south, but they were not supplying nurse midwives to the greater Cincinnati area. Our region had well-established nurse midwifery practices that could support students. These nurse midwives were well qualified as faculty. The community was supportive. Thus, the background and significance section was easy to prepare.

The next section of the training grant describes the curriculum and educational resources. The curriculum is described in detail, including how it fits with the other programs in the educational institution. A paper trail of support for this program is necessary. For the nurse midwifery program, support consisted of a letter from the parent-child health nursing department, the approval from the college curriculum committee, passage of the plan by the faculty, and a letter from the Dean. The local nurse-midwives garnered a letter of support from community obstetricians, the state chapter of the American College of Nurse-Midwives (ACNM), and a consultant who was a nationally recognized nurse midwife and educator. In this type of program, pre-accreditation is necessary from the ACNM and adherence to their core curriculum and competencies is required. Documents to demonstrate attention to these details were submitted with the grant proposal. Detailed recruitment and marketing plans were outlined. A preliminary needs assessment was done to ascertain potential student interest. This document served as the "preliminary studies" that is used in research grants.

Student and graduate data are required. These data must include minority/disadvantaged students. This is a separate table that documents enrollment, attrition, retention, and graduation.

Programs must also demonstrate their adherence to national certification standards. They must show how their curricular plan enables the graduates to take certification, a requirement of employment in many states.

These grants support basic registered nursing programs, special RN mobility programs, advanced training programs (new, expansion, or existing), and unique doctoral programs. Each program offered by a school must have data included on the submitted tables. Having a unique slant on the program such as a doctoral program that addresses rural health care needs and research in this area is an example of a niche program.

Reviewers look at how successful programs are at recruiting and retaining students. Graduation rates are as important as recruitment efforts. Concern is raised if recruitment numbers are high but graduation rates are low. For basic programs, the grant should demonstrate the "Kids Into Healthcare Careers" initiative of the Department of Health and Human Services (DHHS). This initiative puts academic centers in touch with local community middle, junior, and high schools that serve as a conduit for potential nursing students.

Just as the research grants must specify certain elements such as setting, sample, intervention, instruments, data collection, analysis, and timelines, so must the training grant. In the training grant the elements include

- Educational setting and community surrounding the program
- Clinical sites with letters of assurance that they will facilitate student learning
- Curriculum (similar to intervention section in research grant)
- Instruments for data collection
  - Preliminary needs assessment survey data and instrument for collection
  - Student/graduate exit surveys following the program's completion
  - Employer surveys (from institutions that hired past graduates)

The data analysis section of a training grant briefly describes how data are analyzed and used internally to revise programs. The timeline for this grant is just as crucial as for research grants; follow the example given in the research section. Include in this timeline the extra steps that some universities and states require to go before the graduate council of the school or the board of regents at the state level. If this grant represents a completely new program, say a masters program when the school only had an undergraduate program in the past, then regional accreditation must be sought. For example in the state of Ohio, the North Central Accreditation body must sanction new programs. Programs often cannot be accredited until they successfully graduate their first class. Citing these rules and regulations and demonstrating your knowledge of their existence is essential for a successful grant.

Reviewers for these grants usually have expertise in the area of the grant, so know your audience when you write the grant. For example, I review grants for advanced practice training. But my grant review section includes maternal-child, pediatric, and some community-based grants. I do not review all areas of advanced practice nursing. Reviewers serve for more than 1 year in most cases, so if your grant is resubmitted the next year, chances are that at least part of the panel will remember your grant.

The elements of the training grant at the federal level usually include the following:

- Face page
- Table of Contents
- Summary of Proposal—project title, organization, address, project director, project period, program description, number of students and graduates (full and part time); program accreditation (of undergraduate and/or graduate programs), and national certification eligibility.
- Biographical Sketch
- Statements on
  - Assurances—that institution will support this program at the end of the grant period

    - Full-time and Part-time Students (schools must have both unless there is an absolute reason the student must be full time); statement of appointment of the project director-no longer acceptable to state "to be named"
    - Tuition and Fees—must state in-state, out-of-state, full- and part-time costs
    - Enrollment, Graduation, and Traineeship Support Data
    - Required Data
        - Graduate Data—Advanced Education Nursing Traineeship Program, Rural, Underserved, Public Health
        - Minority/Disadvantaged Status Data
        - Faculty Tables—include all faculty, credentials, and the department to which they report
- Funding Factors (if applicable)
    - Statutory Funding Preference (in the request for proposals or program announcements there are statutory funding preferences stated: one must be designated in the proposal); for example, rural health or medically underserved populations
    - Special Consideration Assurance Statement (in the request for proposals or program announcements a special consideration statement is sometimes made). For example, strengthening an existing program of study for individuals with HIV-AIDS. Assurances are made to safeguard discrimination. In applications, assurances or certificates are required that state there is no discrimination in the form of civil rights, handicapped individuals, age, or sex. But a training grant can target a special population such as the elderly or individuals with HIV-AIDS.
- Checklist

Not all educational or training grants are at the federal level. State departments of health or private foundations are other sources of training grant monies. For example, to start our nurse-midwifery program at the University of Cincinnati, the Ohio Department of Health supplied the funds. Another international training program for the University of Cincinnati's Joint Neonatal Nurse and Pediatric Nurse Practitioner Program with Yonsei University was funded in part by the University's Globalization Grant. Another resource we sought for an educational program in Honduras was through the Gates Foundation. A school-based clinic and additional training for the University of Cincinnati's Pediatric Nurse Practitioner students was submitted to a managed care foundation in Cincinnati. Partnerships and alliances with corporations such as hospital corporations are also good sources for monies for such programs. When training grants are submitted to these institutions, the application is usually brief, but contains at least the faculty tables, student tables, and complete description of the educational program.

Special Projects Grants

Special projects grants generally support very specific educational or health care needs. These grants represent special niches. Special Projects of Regional or National

Significance (SPRANS grants), Academic Research Enhancement Award (AREA) program grants, or Centers of Excellence grants are all examples of special projects. This list is not complete, but gives you an idea of the broad range of grants. SPRANS grants must include information on the region or the national initiative to which it is directed. AREA grants, funded through the National Institute of Nursing Research, are available to support new health-related research projects in academic institutions. These grants are small funds aimed to encourage new investigators who might not seek other NIH monies. These funds are designated to support independent studies that will act as a springboard for larger, federally funded programs of research in the future. Special projects grants are a good way for institutions to start to develop research expertise.

The AREA grants are not limited in scope to a specific area of research. For example,

> The National Institute of Allergy and Infectious Diseases (NIAID), National Institute of Diabetes and Digestive and Kidney Diseases (NIDDK), National Institute of Arthritis and Musculoskeletal and Skin Diseases (NIAMS), and the Office of Research on Women's Health (ORWH) invite applications for Autoimmunity Centers of Excellence. The purpose of this cooperative research program is to support integrated basic, pre-clinical and clinical research centers to: conduct single site and multi-site cooperative clinical trials and studies of mechanisms of action of tolerance induction and new immune modulation interventions in multiple autoimmune diseases; accelerate early translation of basic findings into clinical application; facilitate the utilization of clinical materials for basic research studies; enhance the exchange of information between basic scientists and clinicians and among various specialists involved in treating autoimmune diseases; and establish a collaborative approach to clinical and basic research among multiple institutions in various geographic areas. Each Center will include: 1) a clinical component, incorporating multiple clinical specialists to conduct trials and clinical studies of new immunotherapies for autoimmune diseases in cooperation with other Center clinical components, and 2) two or more multidisciplinary, interactive basic and/or pre-clinical research components, focused on elucidation of the basic mechanisms of autoimmunity, self tolerance and/or immune modulation. The basic and clinical components of all Centers will work cooperatively to select, design, and perform the clinical trials/studies and the adjunct basic mechanistic studies. (NIH 2001)

An example of a Center of Excellence in Nursing is the one for Women's Health, established at the University of Illinois at Chicago. There is also Center of Excellence at that University for Narcolepsy.

Cooperative Agreements

Cooperative agreements are just like other types of grants. Some are aimed at education or training, and others are for research or special projects. The difference with cooperative agreements is that the first year of the grant is usually spent outlining, developing, and refining how the grant is to be implemented. The funding agency may have certain programs of education, training, or research already in place at other institutions that they wish the new agency to implement. The protocol used may represent a refinement of one already in place in other sites. A standing protocol for research or education is often supplied by the funding agency for testing in a different population.

The CDC is a good example of an agency that funds cooperative agreements. For example, in the early 1990s they had a request for proposals for fetal alcohol syndrome prevention grants. Those agencies that become funded under this money were asked to work with the CDC to design protocols, data collection instruments, and assessment tools that were used throughout the country and with different populations of pregnant, alcohol-using women. The first year of the grant funding was spent in the development and implementation of the assessment and treatment protocol. Each year of the 5-year grant, all funded project directors were brought together for the purposes of sharing information and working out problems that each agency was encountering.

In this cooperative agreement, the CDC offered services such as statistical consultation to the agencies. The CDC project managers worked closely with their funded projects to make sure that the research was staying on target. These types of arrangements offer less flexibility to the funded project director than a straight research or training grant because the project director must always adhere to the constraints set forth by the funding agency (in this example, the CDC). The benefits are that many of the services needed for successful grant completion are available from the staff of the funding agency. Cooperative agreements can be a win-win situation, especially for the novice grantee; the funding agency works very closely with the local project team. The down side is the lack of flexibility of the protocols due to the need to create a network of research or training that is similar in a variety of settings. Cooperation between the local and federal groups is important if this grant is to work. In the case of the CDC grant, it means that the local research group and community prenatal clinics collaborated closely with the CDC and their research network core groups to decrease alcohol usage in pregnant women for the purpose of preventing fetal alcohol syndrome.

Developing a Timeline for the Grant Writing Project

The previous sections of this chapter related to the elements of a grant, different types of grants, and what the actual process was involved in each step. To be successful, a timeline to follow for the entire grant writing process is necessary. This timeline forms a checklist to determine if your project is on target. Crain and Broome (2000) developed the Grant Application Process Planning Tool (GAPPT) specifically for this purpose. Several universities have used the GAPPT to develop and write successful grants. It provides a rough estimate of the time necessary for each grant writing step. Following this schedule with some adaptation for your unique institutional grant hoops will help you stay on target and meet your grant application deadline (see Appendix D).

Conclusion

There are several aspects that characterize a good grant proposal. First, a good grant proposal is based on a creative, well-articulated, research question and on a significant public health issue. For educational or special projects grant, the proposal must articulate the need and the potential pool of students or persons served. Second, the grant must be methodologically sound, well written, and carefully formatted. The presentation should convince reviewers that the research team is highly knowledgeable about the topic area and possesses the necessary skills in the research methods to expertly carry out the proposed work. Finally, the grant writer must check and recheck the proposal to ensure consistency from specific aims, research questions and hypotheses, background and significance, research design and methods, data analyses, and proposed budget. As a final parting word, do not assume that the reviewers will know what you mean. Putting on the hat of the reviewer versus that of the grant writer may help to clarify issues throughout the proposal that require further explanation.

4 Internal Institutional Process for Grant Writing

Internal Review Process

Each researcher or educational grant writer must determine the mechanism for submitting grants. This statement may seem simple-minded but is an essential, early step in the grant writing process. Many offices and people must sign off on a grant before it is submitted to an Institutional Review Board (IRB) or a funding agency. A timeline is needed for getting these signoffs early in the grant writing process.

Some people find creating a flow sheet or a project timeline helpful. Whatever tool is used, determine what steps are necessary before getting too far into the grant writing process. For example, now that training grants from the Department of Health and Human Services (DHHS) will consider more than one from any institution in a funding cycle, but there should be a compelling reason. This clearinghouse may be a center for nursing research, a department-level committee or chair, or the dean's office.

Next, find out who must approve the grant submission and when. Does the project require submission of a concept paper to a department? A training grant may require that the department or curriculum committee see the proposal before any grant is submitted. If approval by the curriculum committee is necessary, find out how often and when they meet, and how long it will take for final approval. Also carefully read the request for proposals; it may state that a grant must have curriculum, college, or IRB approval prior to submission. For example, The National Institutes of Health (NIH) requires that, once the researchers are notified that their grant is within the fundable range, IRB approval must be sought. The NIH regulations further state that no grant award is released without IRB approval received by NIH in writing.

Early in the grant writing process determine whether a research office or grants office must oversee or approve the project. This office may have staff and support services that would facilitate the grant writing process. Additionally, the grant writing office often serves as the final check of the grant before submission. Who outside the college or institution must sign off? If this is a cooperative agreement or if subcontracts must be drawn up for outside personnel to be hired, determine who does this and how long this process takes as well as what the procedure is for subcontracting. An external agency that is to supply personnel as well as the college or grant writer's own institution often must review a grant before submission.

Does the department head, assistant dean, and/or dean sign off on this project? If so, are any of these persons going to be out of the office for any extended period during the grant development or submission period? How early in the process is their involvement required? Who is responsible for and how is the budget developed? Is this up to the grant writer or is it up to the budget officer or the dean? Does the overall university or hospital administration outside the grant writer's discipline need involvement in the process? If so who, how, at what stage, and how long will this step take?

If personnel or faculty from outside the department or college are used, who has to approve their participation? The person themselves, or their supervisor? This step may require knowledge of the informal as well as formal network in an institution. On occasion, the researcher may encounter individuals who will want or feel they must review the grant prior to its submission but are not found to be in the loop according to the formal institutional organizational chart. Thus, careful and thorough investigation of the appropriate chain of command for giving grant approval is of extreme importance and may prevent the researcher from missing a critical deadline for grant submission.

Identify potential barriers to grant submission. These may be as simple as informally telling a secretary that a grant will be submitted within the next 6 weeks and additional time will need to be set aside for this project. Determine who might provide a letter of support that would influence the grant's success. A person internal or external to your system or a past grant recipient from the funding agency to which you are submitting serves well in this support capacity. Travel or work schedules of these individuals sometimes can hold up a grant if their help is not solicited until the last minute. In grant review panels, the lack of letters of support from key agencies or personnel involved in the grant have been discussion points. Another barrier when it comes to training grant reviews is a lack of evidence of faculty support for curricular changes.

Know the informal and formal politics of who should be notified that a grant is being submitted. For example, as Department Head, I did not like to find out after the fact that a grant was being submitted by one of the departmental faculty without my knowledge. It was not a control issue, but a workforce issue. If there was faculty release time in the grant, I needed to anticipate the possibility of replacing that faculty. If a person is outside your institution and is agreeing to work on your grant, it might be smart to ask if they have talked to their supervisor to make sure internal support is there. If an "expert" in your institution might be upset that you are submitting a grant in their area, consider whether you can work with this person or at least have them write a letter of support for the grant. Better to find out before the grant is submitted that there are going to be problems, than to have problems surface once it is funded.

Another barrier during the summer months for faculty is the unavailability of persons to sign off on grants or to agree to serve on grants. Again, anticipate these scheduling problems early so that you can check vacation schedules and fit them into the grant. Sometimes this is not possible because a grant opportunity suddenly comes up, but in those cases someone can usually cover, at least for signatures. During the summer as well as other times, e-mail letters that only require a revision and signature to those individuals who might be difficult to reach.

Know the timelines for submission to the various departments and IRBs. For example, if you are a doctoral student and on faculty at an institution, you may have to go through an internal review board as a student or faculty prior to the actual submission to, say, a hospital IRB. Know how often these committees meet and what their review cycles are well in advance so these times can be built into the timeline of grant writing. For example, when I did my doctoral dissertation, I had to have my doctoral committee review and approve the proposal (3 weeks), the Associate Dean for Research where I was on faculty (2 weeks), the IRB for the Medical Center where I was a student even though I was not collecting data there (4 weeks), and finally the hospital IRB where the data were collected (4 weeks). The process took almost 4 months. It did help to submit each previous letter of approval to the next IRB. The key word is *plan* and *plan early*!

Conclusion

Planning is the name of the game when it comes to internal institutional grant writing and the submitting process. Know the steps in this process and adhere to them. Always assume this step is going to take twice as long as you expect. This step is important, so don't rush it.

Deadline Dates and Hoops to Jump Through in the Submission Process 5

Grant Jail! The Time Commitment

Unless you have "been there and done that," you have no idea how time consuming grant writing is. Although most of us write grants in between other professional and family responsibilities, the reality is that at some point you must lock yourself up for a few hours or days and just write and rewrite. It feels like grant jail; as you near that submission deadline there are a lot of last minute changes (suggested or mandated Institutional Review Board [IRB] or reviewer revisions) that must be made. This is a time when every 5-minute interruption cannot be tolerated if you plan to get the work done on schedule. Getting some concentrated work time is essential. It may only be 1 to 2 hours but if possible 1 to 2 days, that are strictly devoted to the grant that will make a big difference in the outcome. This writing is not a quick process. Even short grants for foundations (10 pages) require days to actually write a tight, solid grant.

Reviewers Prior to Submission

Try to determine who might be very objective but will give good, constructive criticism on your grant. Have this person or persons read the grant as if they were a peer reviewer. The person may be an expert in the area of the grant that can make sure that you are quoting the most recent researchers or educators in the area (grant reviewers want to make sure you know your grant area and the key names associated with the grant's content area). Another person might review the grant for flow and grammar, and to make sure that you have built a credible case for why your grant should be funded. This person may not have any knowledge of your grant area and be able to tell you that you have not presented enough details to explain the rationale for the grant. An editor can also be helpful in the grant review process by correcting grammar, formatting the application document, designing tables and figures, and checking references.

These reviewers may also include some of the internal people in your institution who must read the grant prior to its submission. Their comments will also help in the peer review process. Of course, at some point you will have to decide how many of the suggestions from reviewers you will include. If the person has been part of a grant review panel, please look carefully at their comments. They know what reviewers look for in grants.

Agency Contact Person for Final Checklist or Technical Support

As stated in Chapter 4, the contact person or technical support staff can be immensely helpful in the grant writing process. Use them and their expertise. They will help you make sure your grant is complete. Use the supplied checklist and, if included, what the review criteria are for the grant reviewers to make sure your application addresses each of these points. Go over and over this checklist before you submit. Ideally, have someone else check the application with you; sometimes you cannot see your own omissions (see Appendix D for a copy of a checklist).

Guidelines: Read, Re-read, and Pray!

Just as with the checklist, go over the actual guidelines for the grant. Review the funding areas, and the key words or objectives that the application packet uses. Use these terms in your grant. It shows the reviewers you read and paid attention to details. If you make a change in one section of the grant, make sure the table or other grant sections that also contain this information are changed as well. Determine whether there are optional tables or sections depending on the type grant you are submitting or the type of institution in which you are working. These are small items that are often overlooked in the grant. Make sure that if someone else is putting your grant together that when the final copies are made, all pages are actually submitted. The copy machine can eat pages, making the grant incomplete and sometimes invalid for review. Once you have done your best to review these items, reviewed the guidelines, and checked the application checklist, put the package in the mail and sit back and pray.

Minority or Other Requested Tables

In many grants today, minority, graduation, or faculty tables are requested. Federal research grants require specific data on the ethnic/racial composition of the setting used for subject recruitment. Tables for educational grants present data on how many minority students are admitted to and have graduated from the institution submitting the grant. Graduation tables contain overall data on the number of students admitted and finally graduated from the various programs the school offers. Faculty tables are used by reviewers to see how many are minority faculty, whether or not they are tenured, how many are full versus part time, the rank of each faculty member, and their areas of expertise. These data help reviewers know if there are enough internal resources and individuals with expertise specified in the grant to support the proposed program, special project, or research. These tables are usually not optional. Make sure they are included. Many grants are now reviewed by sections, such as the purpose and specific aims, the curricular plan, and supporting data. Each section is given so many points. Missing tables can detract from the overall points in the grant. It also suggests to the reviewers that the grant writer does not follow directions or is not detail oriented.

Data to Support Case for Grant

Data to support the rationale for the grant must be detailed enough to let the grant reviewer know that the writer is aware of the national, regional, and local needs and health care trends. For example, if a cancer rehabilitation center is proposed, the rates and types of cancer in Denver may greatly differ from Chicago. This should be reflected in the grant writing. Data need to be current and if no current data are available at one of these levels, then make sure to state that and why. Even an informal needs assessment will strengthen the proposal. Include information on this assessment and how the data were collected. Giving only national data when the grant is administered locally is insufficient to provide a strong rationale for grant funding. Be as specific as you can in terms of each facet of the grant. Give the rationale to support your requests. Do not appear to the reviewers as if you are only trying to add to very adequate resources. Another important aspect is self-sufficiency. If the grant period is 3 years, how are you or your institution going to ensure that this program does not just die at the end of the funding cycle? The self-sufficiency statement, if requested, must be specific, with goals and acknowledgment of potential barriers. The potential barriers should have potential solutions built into the grant even though these are only projected.

Grant Checklist

The grant checklist is the final step in the process. Please review the checklist for submission again and make sure that each item required is included in the packet. The checklist is part of the application packet. The list does vary among funding agencies but the basic elements are essentially the same. Look at the specific mailing instructions given in the packet. Grants mailed to the wrong person or the wrong address are often never reviewed (see Appendix D for a Grant Checklist).

Conclusion

A well-planned submission process will make grant writing much easier. The key is plan, plan, and plan. Be realistic in your timeline for completion. Dedicate time to the actual writing *and* editing of the project. Have it reviewed by others not involved in the grant. Be sure to reexamine your checklist just before the grant is mailed.

Gauging Your Progress: Pink Sheets and Project Reports 6

In this chapter we cover what you need to know about the often-dreaded "Pink Sheets," which inform you of the comments of review committees for federal grants, and any necessary progress reports to the funding agency.

Pink Sheets: Ego Busters or Boosters

The review committees' comments for federal grants comes back to you on "Pink Sheets." Foundations do not always use such a form. The reviewers' comments in any case still hold the same weight. They are either suggesting that your project be funded, revised for resubmission, or rejected. The Pink Sheets, although they are supposed to contain *constructive* criticism, can be very harsh, especially if you have not read one before. They can either bust your ego if your grant appears to the reviewers to be without merit or boost your ego if they really thought your grant was innovative and wonderful. Most grants fall somewhere in the middle.

What You Can Learn

If the review committee did not like your grant, allow yourself a quick pity party and then really read their comments. Was it that you had to submit the grant too quickly or too early in the process? For example, sometimes as educators we are forced, due to budget restraints, to submit a program grant well before the "idea" is really ready. Sometimes your institution includes barriers, such as courses that have little relevance to your proposed program but have been required by the system for decades. In such a case, harsh reviewers' comments may provide impetus for institutional change. So at your ego's expense you may have become a change agent!

Look to see if there is a hidden agenda in the review; perhaps the slant you took on the funding priority is not really congruent with what the foundation was looking for at this time. Perhaps the grant reviewers, and their own areas of expertise, influenced their comments. You may determine you missed subtle cues in their application kit that you could address if given the opportunity to resubmit. Or perhaps it is simply a case of many well-written grants being submitted, but there is not enough money to fund all the really good projects. In this way, even a rejection may not mean that you wrote a bad grant, although it will certainly feel that way at first.

It may be that you are not a good *writer* and that you need technical assistance in the mechanics of grant writing. Most academic and hospital settings provide resources to assist with the grant writing process. Commercial programs are also available that provide proposal master templates that help guide the grant writer through the process.

Regard the review process as a learning experience. If the Pink Sheets are extremely harsh, put them away for a while and then go back to them when you are ready to really read the comments instead of reacting to them. "Try, try again" must be your motto; at the federal level, it generally takes three to four submissions of the same grant before it is actually funded. If you have gotten funded—congratulations—your work has just begun! (See Appendix D for an example of a Pink Sheet.)

Pink Sheets: Conclusion

The dreaded Pink Sheets really provide a lot of good information. The comments, if specific enough, can help you to refine your grant even if it was funded. If the grant was not funded, use the comments to revise the grant for resubmission to the same funding agency or to another one that might be more appropriate.

The Paper Trail for Grant Progess

The same care that you took to write the grant must go into the submission of the progress reports. This section covers the key details of such reports.

Progress Reports Once the Funding Begins

The cycle of these progress reports depends on the funding agency. For some grants, such as Department of Health and Human Services (DHHS) Training grants, these reports are annual noncompeting grant submissions. The acknowledgment of any changes that have occurred during the grant period and the progress made toward meeting the designated objectives/goals must be addressed in these reports. If a particular grant objective has not been met, then clearly state why. Ideally, you should be talking to your technical support person all along the grant's cycle and the agency should already be aware of the problem. Even if they are aware, the problem and possible solution must be included in the report.

In the case of some grants, such as cooperative agreements from the Centers for Disease Control (CDC), quarterly reports are required along with noncompeting grant renewals for each year of the grant. The guidelines for these reports must be followed to comply with the agency's regulations.

Noncompeting Renewal Grants

The funding cycle for a grant is 3 to 5 years for many federal grants. The second, third, and fourth years are referred to as noncompeting grant renewal years. This means that your project team or you, as the project director, is required to resubmit a grant application, including the grant's progress, budget usage or changes, and the proposed activities for the coming year. Because it was previously approved, your grant will not compete with new grant applications for funding. However, if the funding agency is dissatisfied with the grant's progress, they have the option to either decrease the funds or not renew the grant. Grants are rarely terminated, unless there is a very good reason.

This is also the time to request changes in budget lines. You generally need to request it—in writing—any time you need to move monies from one budget line to another before you can actually move the funds. At the time of a noncompeting renewal, however, budgetary changes certainly can be made. It is advisable to discuss the budgetary changes with your contact person at the agency before submitting the request as a part of your noncompeting renewal grant. Be as careful with these applications as you were with the first submission; they will be reviewed and scrutinized in most instances. Today's competitive world dictates an eye for detail in the renewal process.

Timelines for submissions of these reports can be just as sticky as the original grant application. Sometimes an institution has an internal process for how these reports are sent. They may need to be reviewed by the Department Head, Senior Administrator, Comptroller, or Budget Officer. Know these key people, the process, and their time frame for reviewing these reports.

Progress Reports: Conclusion

Maintain the confidence and goodwill of your funding agency by submitting meticulously written, timely reports. When the project director or principal investigator does not follow the guidelines or is habitually late on reports, funding agencies tend to put more pressure on the project. They are concerned about the team's commitment to the project for which they have supported with funds. Do not put yourself in that position. Put your best foot forward and keep on track on the endless paper trail.

When to Look for Further Funding 7

Building a Program of Research or Training

Today, funding is quite competitive, and it is not unusual—especially in academic institutions, teaching hospitals or educational institutions—for researchers or educators to go after funds because they are available, no matter what the topic. Ideally, the researcher or educator should develop a program of related research or educational projects. These projects should continue to build on one another. For example, I had a role in a National Institute on Alcohol and Alcoholism (NIAAA)-funded faculty fellow training grant in the area of substance abuse. As this grant finished, I looked for funding sources in the area of neonatal or perinatal substance abuse. I found a request for proposals from the Centers for Disease Control (CDC) for a cooperative research grant for Fetal Alcohol Syndrome Prevention. In addition to my interest in substance abuse, I had 5 years vested in research concerning "Transition from Hospital to Home" using the neonatal population. I did not want to lose momentum in this area. I had been successful at obtaining small seed grants first for my dissertation from Purdue Frederick Foundation, then from Jewish Hospital, and Rabinowitz Funds from the University of Cincinnati College of Nursing. So I combined the two areas of interest: Fetal Alcohol Syndrome and transition from hospital to home. With the CDC funding I obtained, I was able to continue both areas of research and build a sound foundation of over 10 years of transition research and almost 8 years of substance abuse research. The development of a program of research gained me a good solid network of colleagues in my areas of interest and established my name as being associated with one focused area—perinatal/neonatal/infant research. The focus too helped me obtain March of Dimes monies for educational programs on perinatal substance abuse that would benefit the community and my employer, an academic setting.

The program of research demonstrates a person's ability to focus and not be scattered or take the shotgun approach to research. It affords the researcher more opportunities for dissemination of results as invitations come for presentations and articles in this focus area. It builds a strong package when the researcher/educator/practitioner is going up for tenure or promotion. The person not only presents a track record of funding but also demonstrates a stepwise progression of studies or educational programs.

Expansion of Training or Special Project Grants

The expansion or continuation of training or special projects grants follows primarily the same timelines as a research grant. Basic and Advanced Nursing Education Training Grants are awarded for 3 years with the opportunity to apply during the third year for a continuation of 1 to 2 more years. Special projects grants also follow this pattern. If your program wants to seek an expansion, a strong case for why this should occur must be built. Generally, there is concern that an institution will not continue the program after the federal dollars are gone; a compelling reason for the continuation of the funding is needed. The expansion of the project or grant might include a new population. For example, your first 3 years focused on educating nurses in primary care in the urban setting. This grant was so successful that you now want to expand this education to the rural community by using distance learning and video conferencing. If this is an underserved, underrepresented area in your educational program, then the expansion of the original grant may have merit.

A special project, such as a school-based health clinic for a magnet school, might want to expand its successful model to a very rural middle school to see if the program can educate nurses who will work in the rural community and if community needs are met through this program. Expansion of education- or service-oriented grants is very similar to the research. In each case, you are building a program of either education, practice, or research.

Timeline for Funding the Next Grant

Another aspect of program building is when to seek further funding. Normally, the timeline is dictated by the grant cycle that is currently being followed. In other words, if a grant is for 5 years, then at the beginning of year 4, a new grant should be submitted. Ideally, if funded, the new grant will take over just as the old one is finishing. Another scenario might be that in years 2 or 3 of a 5-year grant, the researcher wants to build in an educational program for faculty, students, or the community. Small grants for this purpose will enhance the current grant and might open other doors for research and educational funding as the original grant period is ending. Timing for future grants is somewhat dictated by the need to bring funds in to support a position. If a person is in a position that they primarily are on soft money (grant dollars) or depend on demonstrating they are bringing in a large portion of their salary, then the timeline for seeking additional funding may have more to do with the institution's financial need than when the original grant funding has ended. The motivator must be considered in relationship to the termination of any grant funds. This motivator will dictate the timeline for future funds.

Conclusion

Timing is everything! This cliché is old but true when in comes to grants. You must plan ahead. Know the funding cycles and when your funds will run out in relationship to these cycles. Start to look for other funds early. Look for unique partnerships for funding—don't just rely on federal dollars to continue to support your work. Remember, you sold your idea once so keep the winning formula going for the next round.

Ethical Dilemmas in Research and Other Grants 8

Ethical Dilemmas

The ethical dilemmas in relationship to research are not new. These came to light when the Tuskeegee Institute was cited for injecting syphilis into prisoners without their knowledge. The Belmont Reports that came out in the 1980s outlined the need for informed consent from any person who is to be involved in research. This and other documents dictate that Institutional Review Boards (IRBs) must review research grants to determine that they are safe and whether the subject's rights are protected. For women and children, it has only been recently that most research could or did include them as research subjects. For women in their childbearing years, the concern was for the possibility that they were pregnant without knowing it and that participating in a study could have deleterious effects on the developing fetus. For children, the concern was whether they might be used as research subjects by their parents when they themselves did not want to participate. There was also the concern that, if a payment for participation was involved, parents would force their children to participate in a study, regardless of the wishes or safety of the children.

Until a child is 11 years old (that is, once they are verbal and have some understanding of whether or not they want to do something), they are usually asked for *assent*, because they are not of legal age to give *consent*. The parents still have to give consent until the age of majority. But what does the researcher do when there is a difference of opinion between the child and parents? No right or wrong answer exists, but this poses an ethical dilemma.

Another dilemma that is becoming more and more common is when funded research and the monies are coming from an industry that desires positive results. Some researchers are getting caught in the bind between reporting actual research results and having to report results that the company wants. This situation is an ethical dilemma. Some researchers are being pushed by these same companies to release findings well before there is much substantiation. This premature release of information can be dangerous if the sample size has been quite small to date.

Ethical dilemmas in research also center on the efficacy of a therapy. When does a researcher stop the experiment? When further variations are no longer being found between subjects? When the therapy is obviously working and the control group is seemingly being denied a potential treatment? When the therapy is obviously not working and to continue might prove harmful to the subjects? Again, all of these situations represent ethical dilemmas. All of them are happening in research worldwide each day. Safeguards must be put into grants that make the grant reviewer know that the researcher is aware of potential biases in the research; that is, the industry dollars funding the project or the potential efficacy of the treatment. It does not mean that a long list of all the possible problems are addressed, but even acknowledgment of when a study might be terminated or how the results (unbiased results) will be disseminated, will help to reassure a review panel that the researcher knows there are potential ethical dilemmas.

Another ethical dilemma involves obtaining information that was not built into the grant. For example, genetic tests are run to determine the presence of the APOE4 gene linked to breast cancer as part of a research project on women's health. In doing these tests, the researcher finds that the variation of APOE4 gene found suggest the person may be at risk for Alzheimer's later in life. What does the researcher do with this information? Is the person told? Is the information withheld? Another version of this same scenario is if additional tests are run with serum or tissue that has been legitimately collected as part of the research and these additional tests, not in the original protocol, reveal a predisposition for a certain condition—what is done with this information? Is the subject or family told? The ethics of performing additional tests is, of course, another facet of the question, but the question of full disclosure of information is a very real ethical dilemma in today's high-tech world. The question sometimes becomes, "Just because we have the technology, should we always use it in research to the maximum?"

The issue that also surrounds these last two cases is that of confidentiality. Who has access to the data that are collected during a research grant? Recently, a large drug store chain was sued because they were able to identify HIV positive patients due to ties with ongoing pharmaceutical research. This chain mailed information to these subjects based on privileged information. The use of such information is a breech of confidentiality; it presents an ethical dilemma for research teams who rely on third parties for equipment, supplies, or medications to do their research. Confidentiality of research participants is also a concern when it comes to employment situations and health insurance coverage. Persons whose names have been inadvertently released due to their participation in research studies have lost their jobs or their families have been denied health insurance. This example is another ethical dilemma secondary to research participation. The best example of this is the early HIV research; when names were associated with a potentially positive HIV status, some participants were denied health insurance or lost coverage and were denied or lost their jobs. Assurances of confidentiality of research participation must be clearly addressed in all grant applications.

Ethical dilemmas are not restricted to research. There are concerns raised with training grants and special projects as to whether or not the confidentiality of data is maintained. Whether participation (or nonparticipation) in the project disadvantages any students or patients is also a concern. If a specific teaching innovation is funded that, 6 months into the project, appears highly successful and increases learning, is it ethical to continue the study? Should this innovation be made available to the other students? This example is but one that can occur in an educational project or a special population project.

Conclusion

Ethical dilemmas are increasing in research, educational, and special projects. The project director must remain sensitive to the potential and real dilemmas. IRBs are in place to assist researchers in analyzing the risk/benefit ratio of the proposed research and to minimize ethical dilemmas that often arise from the conduct of research. Be wary, but not frightened. Be prepared with safeguards for your population.

Life After Grants 9

Beyond the Grant

There really is a life after grants! As a researcher/educator/practitioner, you must decide where you want your career to go after the grant is finished. It may be on to the next project or it may be to take a breather and really think about your next professional move. If you have not been successful at obtaining further funding, then perhaps this is a time to review other avenues for funding with a little different twist. For example, you might seek funds from Avon to examine the use of their skin care products in an adolescent population that has undergone chemotherapy with resultant dry skin. Or you might look at the use of complementary therapies in the treatment of women with endometriosis who are infertile. Although these two areas may not seem to out of line with current trends, they are not the usual mode of research for most nurses; the "twist" might give you a competitive edge. Another example is a nurse researcher with fibromyalgia who wants to compare time to diagnosis between non-health professionals and professionals. Again, this idea is not far from mainstream, but has a new twist and may produce cost-effective results if one group is determined to obtain a diagnosis of fibromyalgia sooner than the other.

The time after a grant also affords you space to get the manuscripts and presentations written that seemed so elusive during the day-to-day administration of the grant. Presentations can be a joy when they come from your passion. Tell your story. Get people excited about you and your work. These presentations can also bring you into contact with other researchers or persons responsible for funding in your area. Remember that these presentations are selling your expertise and your work. A well-articulated presentation will bring other opportunities for success. These opportunities may take your career in a slightly different direction than you had planned. Don't be afraid to go for the ride!

Don't underestimate the power of poster presentations. Many seasoned researchers or educators will not do posters. Personally, I find them very rewarding because novices will ask many questions when you are standing by a poster; few will ask these questions in a large audience listening to an oral presentation. For the seasoned researcher, this is a time to be a good role model and help shape the career of a junior researcher. You can provide mentorship to another person. If you are the novice researcher or educator, a poster presentation is less intimidating than standing before the masses to orally present.

Take this time to renew your life. Too many times, nurses in particular try to continue to do it all. Let's face it: a grant and the work associated with it takes its toll on our lives and those of our family and friends. The time after a grant lets you renew your ties with the outside world. Some of you may laugh at that statement, but others know this to be true of either yourself or some of your colleagues. So take the time. Take that vacation. Go to that play you have been putting off for months. Renew your soul so you are ready for the next project.

Conclusion

Take time. Take care. Life does go on and really is not grant dependent. You are finally out of grant jail! Take advantage of the break. You earned it!

References

Bayley, N. 1969. *Bayley's Scales of Infant Development.* New York: Psychological Corp.

Beyea, S., and L.H. Nicoll. 1998. Debunking research myths—Research on a shoestring budget. *Association of Operating Room Nurses Journal* 68(2): 284–287.

Beyea, S., and L.H. Nicoll. 1998. Finding research funding sources. (Research Corner). *Association of Operating Room Nurses Journal* 68(3): 462, 464, 466.

Birkett, N.J. 1994. The review process for applied-research grant proposals. Suggestions for revisions. *Canadian Medical Association Journal* 150(8): 1227–1229.

Black, N. 1998. The pocket guide to grant applications. (Book Review). *British Medical Journal* 316(8136): 1029.

Brakey, M.R. 1997. Tips for the novice grantseeker: Implications for staff development specialists. *Journal of Nursing Staff Development* 13(3): 160–163.

Canadian Palliative Care Association 1995. *Canadian Palliative Care Association: Palliative Care: Towards A Consensus In Standardized Principles Of Practice.* Ontario, Canada: Canadian Palliative Care Association.

Carden, D.L., S. Dronene, G. Gehrig, and R.J. Zalenski. 1998. Funding strategies for emergency medicine research. *Annals of Emergency Medicine* 31(2): 179–187.

Corff, K., R.. Seideman, P. Venkataraman, L. Lutes, and B. Yates. 1995. Facilitated tucking: A nonpharmacologic comfort measure for pain in preterm neonates. *Journal of Obstetrics, Gynecology, & Neonatal Nursing* 24(2): 143–147.

Crain, H.C. and M.E. Broome. 2000. Tool for planning the grant application process. *Nursing Outlook* 48(6): 288–293.

DHHS (Department of Health and Human Services). 2001. www.hhs.gov

Fuller, E.O., E.G. Hasselmeyer, J.C. Hunter, F.G. Abdellah, and A.S. Hinshaw. 1991. Summary statements of the NIH Nursing Research Grant Applications. *Nursing Research* 40(6): 346–351.

Gaaberson, K.B. 1997. What's the answer? What's the question. *Association of Operating Room Nurses Journal* 66(1): 148–151.

Grunau, R., M., Whitfield, and J. Petrie. 1994. Pain sensitivity and temperament in extremely low-birth-weight premature toddlers and preterm and full-term controls. *Pain* 58: 341–346.

Hazeldine, J. 1982. Bayley scales of infant development. In Humenick, S.S. (ed). *Analysis of Current Assessment Strategies in the Health Care of Young Children and Childbearing Families.* Norwalk, CT: Appleton-Century-Crofts.

Horrobin, D.F. 1996. Peer review of grant applications: A harbinger for mediocrity in clinical research? *The Lancet* 348(9037): 1293–1295.

Horton, R. 1996. Luck, lotteries, and loopholes of grant review. *The Lancet* 48(9037): 1255–1256.

Jones C.B., L. Tulman, and C.M. Clancy. 1999. Research funding opportunities at the Agency for Health Care Policy and Research. *Nursing Outlook* 47(4): 156–161.

Kachoyeanos, M.K. 1998. Developing the research protocol. *Maternal Child Nursing (MCN)* 23: 273.

Kachoyeanos, M.K. 1997. Research funding sources. *Maternal Child Nursing (MCN)* 22(6): 323–324.

Kahn, C.R. 1994. Picking a research problem—The critical decision. *The New England Journal of Medicine* 330(21): 1530–1533.

Kenner, C. 1991. *Perinatal Alcohol Users: Identification and Intervention.* Grant funded by the Centers for Disease Control and Prevention, Atlanta, GA.

Krammer, L.M., J.C. Muir, N. Gooding-Kellar, M.B.Williams, and C.F. von Gunten. 1999. Palliative care and oncology: Opportunities for oncology nursing. *Oncology Nursing Updates,* 6: 1–12.

Krammer, L.M., A.A. Ring, J. Martinex, M.J. Jacobs, and M.B. Williams. 2001. The nurse's role in interdisciplinary and palliative care. In Matzo, M.L. and D.W. Sherman (eds.). *Palliative Care Nursing: Quality Care To The End Of Life.* New York: Springer, pp. 118-139.

Kroenke, K. 1996. Conducting research as a busy clinician-teacher or trainee: Starting blocks, hurdles, and finish lines. *Journal of General Internal Medicine* 11(6): 360–365.

Locke, L.F., W.W. Spirduso, and S.J. Silverman (eds.). 1993. *Proposals That Work: A Guide for Planning Dissertations and Grant Proposals,* 3rd ed. Newbury Park, CA: Sage.

Lorentzon, M. 1995. Multidisciplinary collaboration: Lifeline for drowning pool for nurse researchers? *Journal of Advanced Nursing* 22(5): 825–826.

Malone, R.E. 1996. Getting your study funded: Tips for new researchers *Journal of Emergency Nursing* 22(5): 457–459.

Masis, K.B., and P.A. May. 1991. A comprehensive local program for the prevention of fetal alcohol syndrome. *Public Health Reports* 106(6): 484–489.

Moody, L.E. 1990 *Advancing Nursing Science Through Research,* Vol 1. Newbury Park, CA: Sage.

Moody, L.E. 1990. Randomized clinical control trials. In Moody, L.E. (ed). *Advancing Nursing Science Through Research,* Vol 2. Newbury Park, CA: Sage, p. 19.

National Institutes of Health. 2001. Request for Applications, 2001, www.grants.nih.gov/grants/guide/rfa-files/RFA-AI-98-010.html

NIAAA. 1990. *Alcohol Alert. Screening for Alcohol.* No. 8, PH285, Rockville, MD: National Institute on Alcohol Abuse and Addiction.

NINR. 2001. www.ninr.gov

Patterson, E.R., and S. Bakewell-Sachs. 1998. Toward evidence-based practice. *Maternal Child Nursing (MCN)* 23: 278–280.

Polit, D., and B.P. Hungler. 1998. *Nursing Research: Principles and Methods.* Philadelphia: Lippincott, Williams & Wilkins.

Ries, J.B., and C.G. Leukefeld. 1995. *Applying for Research Funding: Getting Started and Getting Funded.* London: Sage.

Schwinn, D.A., E.R. DeLong, and S.L. Safer. 1998. Writing successful research proposals for medical science. *Anesthesiology* 88(6): 1660–1666.

Streubert, H.J., and D.R. Carpenter. 1995. Philosophical dimensions of qualitative research. In Streubert, H.J., and D.R. Carpenter (eds): *Qualitative Research in Nursing: Advancing the Humanistic Imperative.* Philadelphia: J.B. Lippincott, p. 12.

Tornquist, E. 1986. *From Proposal to Publication: An Informal Guide to Writing About Nursing Research.* Menlo Park, CA: Addison-Wesley.

Tornquist, E., and S. Funk. 1990. How to write a research grant proposal. *IMAGE* 22(1): 44–51.

Walden, M. 2000. Area grant application. *Environmental and Sleep On Preterm Infant's Pain Response.* Washington, DC: National Institute for Nursing Research.

Wessely, S. 1998. Peer review of grant applications. What do we know? *The Lancet* 325(9124): 301–305.

Glossary A

Academic Research Enhancement Award (AREA)—Monies used to support new investigators in a specific area of research. The purpose is to help investigators begin an independent research career in a focused area.

Cooperative agreement—This form of grant usually requires the grantee and grantor work together after the funding begins to formulate research protocols.

Direct costs—Expenses, such as salaries, equipment specifically designated for the project, and other monies that go to support the actual project.

Evidence-based practice—The use of scientific data or a large collection of practical knowledge that support clinical interventions.

GANTT chart—A visual use of bar graphs to depict timelines for various aspects of a project.

Indirect costs—The expenses or overhead that it takes to run a grant: the benefits packages, cost of utilities, phone cost, and other "hidden costs" that are part of the bricks and mortar of conducting daily business in any institution.

Institutional Review Board (IRB)—A review panel made up of health professionals and at least one or two laypersons that examines the grant for research safety and scientific merit only in relationship to participant rights and safety. This panel resides either in the hospital where the research, educational, or special project is conducted, in the academic center, or both.

Noncompeting renewal grant—A resubmission of an ongoing grant that will not be considered against a new applicant pool of grants for that year. It is not competing for the dollars for that grant year along with new grants. Funds for this grant were designated for multiple years. However, the renewal of the grant is predicated on solid evidence that the grant is doing what it set out to do. Dollars can be decreased or withdrawn if no real progress is shown in the grant reports or renewal.

Pink Sheets—At the federal level, critiques have in the past been printed on pink sheets, but are no longer always pink. These sheets provide critiques of the proposed project. The comments list strengths, weaknesses, summary, and recommendations for funding.

Request for Applications (RFA)—A call for grantees to apply for research or educational funds. These calls designate the objectives for the grant monies, the type of grant that will be accepted for review, and the cycle for the grant from application to the funding announcement.

Request for Proposals (RFP)—This is another name for the call for grant applications. It is basically the same as a RFA, but applications are accepted on a broad range of research priorities versus solicitation of proposals for a specific designated priority area.

Special Projects of Regional or National Significance (SPRANS)—Grant funds to support projects that support a regional or national health care need.

Power analysis—A method by which a sample size is calculated to achieve significance. This analysis considers the level of significance of the variable of interest, the effect size desired, and finally what number of subjects it will take to achieve significance results.

Qualitative research—A method of research that looks at the subjective world view. The concern is to describe "what is" rather than be able to predict why an event occurred.

Quantitative research—A research method interested in quantifying or counting responses. This type of research answers questions of relationships, probability, causality, and predictability. Objective, verifiable data are of interest.

Systematic or integrated reviews—Reviews of literature, usually of randomized clinical control trials, that represent the state of the science on a specific topic. Databases on the Internet house these reviews that provide evidence to support a grant area or an intervention.

Resources: Printed or Web Based B

A plethora of grant resources are available through the print media or the Internet. This list is not meant to be all inclusive, but to give a start to early search efforts. Listing of a resource does not imply an endorsement of the institution.

Grant Funding Sources for Health Care Subjects

The following list represents foundations and other funding agencies that support research, education, scholarships, or special projects. The funding areas listed will help you to determine exactly what type of project each agency supports.

American Nurses Foundation

600 Maryland Avenue, SW
Suite 100 W
Washington, DC, 20024-2571
Grants voicemail: (202) 651-7298
ANF@ana.org or www.nursingworld.org/anf/99grant.htm

Funding Areas

Beginning and advanced nurse researchers who are developing a research career. There are several co-sponsored grants that have a specific area of nursing research that is specified; otherwise funds are available for general nursing research.

Archstone Foundation

401 East Ocean Boulevard, Suite 1000
Long Beach, CA, 90802
Phone: (562) 590-8655
Fax: (562) 495-0317
E-mail: archstone@archstone.org
www.archstone.org

Funding Areas

Health and well-being of seniors and supporting their choices in health care throughout the aging process. The majority of grants support senior programs in Southern California. Demonstration projects and programs that have a regional or national impact on senior issues are considered from any part of the country.

Association for Women's Health Obstetrics, and Neonatal Nursing (AWHONN)

2000 L Street, NW
Suite 740
Washington, DC 20036
Phone: (800) 673-8499 (US)
Phone: (800) 245-0231 (Canada)
Fax: (202) 728-0575
http://www.awhonn.org/

Funding Areas

Small Research Grants Program: Seed monies for pilot research or funding for small projects that focus on women's health or newborn care. Many of these awards are through corporate sponsorship.

Agilent Technologies: Improving Health for Women and Newborns with Technology: research must include technology.

Hill-Rom Maternal Child Investigator: Research must center on maternal child nursing.

Johnson & Johnson Marshall Klaus Mother Baby: Focus is on maternal child nursing.

Wyeth-Ayerst Women's Health Investigator: Research must concern women's health issues.

Grant for Research in Women's Health Care: The Jacobs Institute of Women's Health: Support new, innovative methods of health care delivery of women's health services.

Dannon Institute Research Program: The focus is on nutrition and can include postdoctorates in the areas of nutrition and community nutrition.

Verizon Foundation (formerly Bell Atlantic Foundation)

1095 Avenue of the Americas
New York, NY 10036
Phone: (800) 621-9900 or (212) 395-2121
E-mail: webmaster@verizon.com
www.foundation.verizon.com

Funding Areas

Best in Class-Model Technology Grants in Delaware, Maine, Maryland, Massachusetts, New Hampshire, New Jersey, New York, Pennsylvania, Rhode Island, Vermont, Virginia, Washington, DC, and West Virginia.

Priority is technology integration. Main areas of interest are literacy, digital divide, workforce development, employee volunteerism, and community technology development. These funds are disseminated for program and research efforts.

Centers for Disease Control and Prevention (CDC)

1600 Clifton Road
Atlanta, GA 30333
Phone: (404) 639-3311 or (404) 639-3534 or (800) 311-3435
www.cdc.gov/ or www.cdc.gov/od/pgo/funding/funding.htm or
www.cdc.gov/od/pgo/forminfo.htm

Funding Areas

Multiple program and research grant opportunities exist with the CDC:

1. Agency for Toxic Substances and Disease Registry Public Health Conference Support Grant Program
2. *HIV Prevention Projects*: HIV/AIDS Surveillance and HIV Incidence and Prevalence Surveys; Leadership and Investment in Fighting an Epidemic (LIFE)-Global AIDS Activity; National Partnerships for Human Immunodeficiency Virus (HIV) Prevention With a Focus on Business and Labor, Youth-at-High Risk, and Migrant Workers; Public Health Conference Support Cooperative Agreement Program for Human Immunodeficiency Virus (HIV) Prevention.
3. *Chronic Disease Prevention/Health Promotion*: Post-Infective Fatigue: A Model for Chronic Fatigue Syndrome; Health Promotion and Disease Prevention Initiatives Related to Chronic Disease Prevention and Health Promotion; Initiative to Educate State Legislatures about Priority Public Health Issues
4. *Emerging Infections*: Epidemiology and Laboratory Capacity for Infectious Diseases
5. *Environmental Health*: Childhood Lead Poisoning Prevention Programs
6. *Injury and Violence Prevention and Control*: Grants for Acute Care; Rehabilitation and Disability Prevention Research; Grants for Traumatic Injury Biomechanics Research; Grants for Violence-Related Injury Prevention Research
7. *Minority Health/Health Promotion*
8. *Occupational Safety and Health*: Beryllium-Induced Diseases; Occupational Safety and Health R01's; Research Methods for Occupational Cancer; State Fatality Surveillance and Field Investigations of Occupational Injuries: Fatality Assessment and Control Evaluation; Career Development Grants in Occupational Safety and Health Research (K01's); Small Grants in Occupational Safety and Health Research (R03's); Community-Based Interventions to Prevent Childhood Agricultural Injury and Disease; World-Wide Occupational Safety and Health Program; Centers for Agricultural Disease and Injury Researcher, Education and Prevention; Traumatic Occupational Injury

Research: Science for Prevention; Extended Work Schedules in the New Economy: Health and Safety Risks to Workers; Occupational Exposure to Putative Reproductive/Developmental Toxicants in Humans

9. *Public Health Laws and Practices*: Association of State and Territorial Directors of Health Promotion and Public Health Education (ASTDHPPHE)
10. *Sexually Transmitted Diseases*: Competitive Supplemental Funds for Comprehensive STD Prevention Systems: Monitoring STD Prevalence and Reproductive Health Services for Adolescent Women in Special Settings
11. *Tuberculosis*

CDC Foundation

50 Hurt Plaza
Suite 765
Atlanta, GA 30303
Phone: (404) 653-0709 or (888) 880-4CDC [(888) 880-4232]
Fax: (404) 653-0330
www.cdcfoundation.org/index1.shtml

Funding Areas

Price Fellowships for HIV Prevention: builds relationships between governmental and nongovernmental agencies to provide HIV prevention programs. Grants are given to support information programs that build partnerships to promote health.

China Foundation

International Office: 9216 Falls Chapel Way
Potomac, MD 20854
Phone: (301) 340-2065
Fax: (301) 340-3814
E-mail: info@chinafoundation1.org or education@chinafoundation1.org, or health@chinafoundation1.org
www.chinafoundation1.org/

Funding Areas

Think tank to support health care, education, and social security reform in China. Projects that provide basic medical services to remote China villages, renovation or building of elementary China schools, or working with other nonprofit organizations, foundations, and think tanks to develop and improve health care systems, health insurance, education, and environmental protection for China.

The Commonwealth Fund

One East 75th Street
New York, NY 10021-2692

Phone: (212) 606-3800
Fax: (212) 606-3500
E-mail: nb@cmwf.org
www.commonwealthfund.org/fellowships/index.asp

Funding Areas

Research on health and social policy issues.

Fellowship Programs

The Commonwealth Fund/Harvard University Fellowship in Minority Health Policy; Harkeness Fellowships in Health Care Policy; and Ian Axford Fellowships in Public Policy.

Program Grants

Research on health and social issues with emphasis on practice and policy. The fund is most concerned about vulnerable populations. Specific programs areas are improving access to care, improving quality of health care services, international health care policy and practice, and improving public spaces and services.

Charles E. Culpeper Foundation and the Rockefeller Brothers Fund

These funds have merged.

437 Madison Avenue, 37th Floor
New York, NY 10022-7001
Phone: (212) 812-4200
Fax: (212) 812-4299
E-mail: rock@rbf.org
www.rbf.org/

Funding Areas

Health, education, arts and culture, and administration of justice.

Nathan Cummings Foundation

1926 Broadway
Suite 600
New York, NY 10023-6915
Phone: (212) 787-7300
Fax: (212) 787-7377
E-mail: grants@cummings.ncf.org
www.ncf.org/

Funding Areas

Environment, health, Jewish life, spirituality, and democratic values.

Department of Health and Human Services (DHHS)

Grants Management Branch
Bureau of Health Professions
Health Resources and Services Administration
8C-26 Parklawn Building
5600 Fishers Lane
Rockville, MD 20857
www.hrsa.dhhs.gov/bhpr/

Funding Areas

Academic administrative units in primary care, predoctoral training in primary care, physician assistant training in primary care, advanced education nursing grants, advanced education nursing traineeship grants, advanced education nursing-nurse anesthetist traineeship grant program, residency training in primary care, faculty development in primary care, residencies in the practice of pediatric dentistry, residencies and advanced education in the practice of general dentistry, basic nurse education and practice grants, and public health nursing experiences in state and local health departments for baccalaureate nursing.

Friends Research Institute, Inc.

505 Baltimore Avenue
PO Box 10676
Baltimore, MD 21285
Phone: (410) 823-5116
Fax: (410) 823-5131
www.friendsresearch.org/

Funding Areas

Research for medical, drug, mental treatments, and pharmaceutical studies.

Foundation for Neonatal Research and Education

c/o Anthony J. Jannetti, Inc.
Box 56
Pitman, NJ 08071-0056
Phone: (856) 256-2300
Fax: (856) 589-7463
www.ajj.com

Funding Areas

Neonatal health care issues. Application of research to neonatal practice.

Fullbright Scholar Program

Institute of International Education
809 United Nations Plaza

New York, NY 10017-3580
E-mail: info@iie.org
www.iie.org/fulbright/

Funding Areas

Fellowships and programs aimed at university coursework, independent library or field research, classes in a music conservatory or art school, special projects in the social or life sciences, or a combination. The scholarships can be for US International Students and Scholars, part of faculty/student exchanges.

Bill and Melinda Gates Foundations

William H. Gates Foundation
PO Box 23350
Seattle, WA 98102
www.gatesfoundation.org

Funding Areas

Innovations in education, technology, and world health. Special emphasis on use of technology in third world countries. Health care, health promotion, and other health-related issues involving technology for education or care delivery are acceptable areas.

John Simon Guggenheim Memorial Foundation

90 Park Avenue
New York, NY 10016
Phone: (212) 6897-4470
Fax: (212) 697-3248
E-mail: fellowships@gf.org
www.gf.org

Funding Areas

Fellowships for advanced professionals in all fields except performing arts.

Walter and Elise Haas Fund

One Lombard Street
Suite 305
San Francisco, CA 94111-1130
Phone: (415) 398-4474
Fax: (415) 986-4779
E-mail: Brenda@haassr.org
www.haassr.org/

Funding Areas

Leadership development.

Health Resources and Services Administration (HRSA)

8C-26 Parklawn Building
5600 Fishers Lane
Rockville, MD 20857
Phone: (877) HRSA-123
Grants Application Center
E-mail: hrsagac@hrsa.gov
www.hrsa.dhhs.gov/grants.htm

Funding Areas

This is the Bureau of Primary Health Care, the Bureau of Health Professions, Bureau of Maternal and Child Health, and HIV/AIDS Bureau. Funding areas are education and training of health professionals. See DHHS for more information.

Howard Hughes Medical Institute

4000 Jones Bridge Road
Chevy Chase, MD 20815-6789
Phone: (301) 215-8500
E-mail: webmaster@hhmi.org/
www.hhmi.org/

Funding Areas

Strengthening science education from kindergarten through graduate school. Graduate program awards for graduate education and medical student research training fellowships. Biomedical research is also supported.

Institute of Medicine Office of Health Policy Programs and Fellowships

Marion Ein Lewin
Office of Health Policy
Programs and Fellowships
2101 Constitution Avenue, NW
Washington, DC 20418
Phone: (202) 334-1506
E-mail: iomwww@nas.edu
www.nas.edu/iom/hppf/hppfhome.nsf

Funding Areas

Advancement of scientific knowledge to improve health.

International Research & Exchanges Board

1616 H Street, NW
6th Floor
Washington, DC 20006

Phone: (202) 628-8188
Fax: (202) 628-8189
E-mail: irex@irex.org
www.irex.org/

Funding Areas

Exchange of US Scholars to conduct research in Central and Eastern Europe (CEE), the New Independent States (NIS), Mongolia, and China.

Ittleson Foundation

Anthony C. Wood, Executive Director
Ittleson Foundation, Inc.
15 East 67th Street
New York, NY 10021
Phone: (212) 794-2008
www.IttlesonFoundation.org/

Funding Areas

Resources for organizations that serve the environment, those with AIDS, and those with mental health problems.

W.M. Keck Foundation

555 South Flower Street
Suite 3230
Los Angeles, CA 90071
Phone: (213) 680-3833
E-mail: webmaster@wmkeck.org
www.wmkeck.org/

Funding Areas

Grants in the areas of medical research and science. Liberal arts colleges and selected community services are also supported.

W.K. Kellogg Foundation

One Michigan Avenue East
Battle Creek, MI 49017-4058
Phone: (616) 968-1611
Fax: (616) 968-0413
www.wkkf.org/

Funding Areas

Building the capacity of individuals, communities, and institutions to solve their own problems.

Lymphoma Research Foundation of America, Inc.

8800 Venice Boulevard, #207
Los Angeles, CA, 90034
Phone: (310) 204-7040
Fax: (310) 204-7043
E-mail: LRFA@aol.com
www.lymphoma.org/

Funding Areas

Research and providing patient resources, including support groups, educational materials, clinical trials, information, and a periodic newsletter.

A.L. Mailman Family Foundation

707 Westchester Avenue
White Plains, NY 10604
Phone: (914) 681-4448
Fax: (914) 686-5519
E-mail: betty@mailman.org
www.mailman.org/

Funding Area

Children and families, with a special emphasis on early childhood.

Priorities

Infant/toddler care, professional development and compensation, quality, advocacy, strengthening diverse leadership.

Magic Johnson Foundation, Inc.

600 Corporate Pointe
Suite 1080
Culver City, CA 90230
Phone: (888) MAGIC-05 or (888) 624-4205
www.magicjohnson.org/

Funding Areas

Community-based organizations serving the health, educational, and social needs of children residing in inner-city communities. This is a for-profit group that provides grant consultants and proposal writers. Their mission is to provide the finest grants consulting service available.

March of Dimes Birth Defects Foundation

1275 Mamaroneck Avenue
White Plains, NY 10605

Phone: (888) MODIMES [663-4637]
www.modimes.org/

Funding Areas

Educational programs related to maternal-child health; innovative programs and research projects that concern prevention of birth defects.

McGovern Family Foundation

The Terry McGovern Foundation
Janine L. Clarke, Executive Director
PO Box 33393
Washington, DC 20033
Phone: (202) 463-8750
E-mail: jeffjay@terrymcgovern.org
www.mcgovernfamily.org/

Funding Areas

Research into alcoholism, to assist in fundraising for treatment and recovery, and to increase public understanding of addiction.

Merrill Lynch Forum: The Innovation Grants Competition

c/o Katia Mujica Communications & Public Affairs
2 World Financial Center, Floor #6
New York, NY 10281-6106
Phone: (888) 33-FORUM
E-mail: InnovationGrants@ml.com
www.merlyn.com/woml/forum/innovation/

Funding Areas

Doctoral students whose topic could be converted into a commercial product/service.

National Hospice Foundation

1700 Diagonal Road
Suite 300
Alexandria, VA 22314
Phone: (703) 516-4928
Fax: (703) 525-5762
E-mail: info@nhpco.org
www.nho.org/foundation.htm

Funding Areas

Increasing awareness of and access to hospice care education and research.

National Institutes of Health

Center for Scientific Review
6701 Rockledge Drive, Room 1040-MSC 7710
Bethesda, MD 30892-7710 or Bethesda, MD 20917 (for express/courier service)
Grantsinfo
National Institutes of Health
Phone: (301) 435-0714
Fax: (301) 480-0525
E-mail: grantsinfo@nih.gov
www.grants.nih.gov/grants/

Funding Areas and Priorities

These are all found in the NIH Guide Notice available through grantsinfo@nih.gov. All forms of research regarding health-related issues are funded. Each institute lists funding priorities.

The National Science Foundation

4201 Wilson Boulevard
Arlington, VA 22230
Phone: (703) 306-1234 or (800)-877-8339
E-mail: info@nsf.gov
www.nsf.gov/home/grants.htm

Funding Areas

Broad areas that include education, research, and small businesses. Areas include biology, computer and information sciences, crosscutting programs, education, engineering, geosciences, international, math, physical sciences, polar research, science statistics, and social and behavioral sciences.

New England Biolabs Foundation

Martine Kellett, Executive Director
32 Tozer Road
Beverly, MA 01915
Phone: (978) 927-2404
Fax: (978) 921-1350
Fax e-mail: kellett@nebf.org
E-mail inquiries should go to: cataldo@nebf.org
www.nebf.org/

Funding Areas

Supports grassroots organizations working with the environment, social change, the arts, elementary education, and scientific research.

Onassis Public Benefit Foundation

Alexander S. Onassis Public Benefit Foundation
Athens 7 Eschinou str.
GR 105 58, Athens, Greece
Phone: (+301) 37 13 000
Fax: (+301) 37 13
www.onassis.gr/

Funding Areas

Scholarships and research grants, international competitions.

David and Lucille Packard Foundation

300 Second Street, Suite 200
Los Altos, CA 94022
Phone: (650) 948-7658
www.packfound.org/

Funding Areas

Supports universities, community groups, national institutions, and community agencies. They publish *The Future of Children.*

Pew Charitable Trusts

2005 Market Street, Suite 1700
Philadelphia, PA 19103-7077
E-mail: info@pewtrusts.com
www.pewtrusts.com/

Funding Areas

A portion of the annual grant-making budget is dedicated to serving the needs of the Philadelphia community in the areas of culture, education, environment, health and human services, public policy, and religion.

RGK Foundation

Gregory A. Kozmetsky, President
RGK Foundation
1301 West 25th Street, Suite 300
Austin, TX 78705-4236
Phone: (512) 474-9298
Fax: (512) 474-7281
www.rgkfoundation,org

Funding Areas

Medical, educational, and community programs and research.

Sarnoff Endowment for Cardiovascular Science, Inc.

731 G-2 Walker Road
Great Falls, VA 22066
Phone: (888) 4-SARNOFF
Fax: (703) 759-7838
www.sarnoffendowment.org/

Funding Areas

Medical students to perform 1 year of research in the cardiovascular sciences at an institution other than their own.

Sigma Theta Tau International

550 West North Street
Indianapolis, IN 46202
Phone: (317) 634-8171 or (317) 634-8171 or (888) 634-7575
Fax: (317) 634-8188
E-mail: stti@stti.iupui.edu
www.nursingsociety.org/

Funding Areas

Virginia Henderson Clinical Research Grant: Clinical issues
Rosemary Berkel Crisp Research Award: women's health, oncology, and infant/child care
Mead Johnson Nutritionals Research Grant: nutrition and health
Small Grants: no specific target area

The Society of Pediatric Nursing

7794 Grow Drive
Pensacola, FL 32514-7072
Phone: (800) 723-2902
Fax: (850) 484-8762
www.pednurse.org/

Funding Areas

Grants for research and education that focus on children's health.

Paul and Daisy Soros Fellowships for New Americans

Warren F. Ilchman, Director
400 West 59th Street
New York, NY 10019
Phone: (212) 547-6926
Fax: (212) 548-4623

E-mail: pdsoros_fellows@sorosny.org
www.pdsoros.org

Funding Areas

Graduate study for new Americans.

Spencer Foundation

875 North Michigan Avenue
Suite 3930
Chicago, IL 60611-1803
Phone: (312) 337-7000
Fax: (312) 337-0282
www.spencer.org/.

Funding Area

Faculty research and fellowships that contribute to the understanding and improvement of education.

The Stuart Foundation

50 California Street
Suite 3350
San Francisco, CA 9411-4735
Phone: (415) 393-1551
Fax: (415) 393-1552
www.stuartfoundation.org/

Funding Areas

Help children and youth of California and Washington states become responsible citizens. The three programs of support are Strengthening the Public School System, Strengthening the Child Welfare System, and Strengthening Communities to Support Families.

Priorities

Policy analysis and development; stronger connections among policy makers, practitioners, and researchers; collaboration across agencies and disciplines; building public understanding of key issues in community well-being; improving practice, innovations/demonstrations; and dissemination.

Texas A & M Research Foundation

Box 3578 TAMUS
College Station, Texas 77843
Mail Stop 3578

Dulie Bell Building
Corner of University and Wellborn Drives
Phone: (979) 845-8600
Fax: (979) 845-7143
E-mail: webmaster@rf-mail.tamu.edu
www.rf-web.tamu.edu/

Funding Areas

Provides network on developments in funding sources, sponsor requirements, and regulations.

Weingart Foundation

1055 West Seventh Street
Los Angeles, CA 90017-2305
Phone: (213) 688-7799
Fax: (213) 688-1515
E-mail: info@weingartfnd.org
www.weingartfnd.org/

Funding Areas

Grants to human service organizations, educational and health institutions, and cultural centers throughout Southern California.

White House Fellowships

The President's Commission on White House Fellowships
712 Jackson Place NW
Washington, DC 20503
Phone: (202) 395-4522
Fax: (202) 395-6179
E-mail: info@whitehousefellows.gov
www.whitehousefellows.gov

Funding Areas

Provides gifted and highly motivated young Americans some firsthand experience in the process of governing the nation. Nurses are included in this group. This fellowship is an excellent opportunity for gaining first hand knowledge of policy making

US DHHS Resources and Other Governmental Agencies

These agencies of the federal government often support research, education, some educational scholarships, and special projects themselves or have links to agencies that do. They are a good resource for gaining information for a grant's background and significance section.

- Adolescent pregnancy program: www.hhs.gov/opa/titlexx/oapp
- Adoption: www.acf.dhhs.gov/programs/cb
- Adoption/abductions: www.travel.state.gov
- Aging-Eldercare information and research: www.aoa.dhhs.gov
- AIDS/HIV: Prevention, testing, treatment, and prevention information: www.cdc.gov/dstd/dstdp.html
- Alcohol: www.niaaa.nih.gov
- Alcohol/drug: www.nida.nih.gov
- Arthritis/bone diseases: www.nih.gov/niams
- Autism: www.ninds.nih.gov
- Birth defects: www.nih.gov/nichd
- Blindness/eye information: www.nei.nih.gov
- Brain tumors: www.nci.nih.gov
- Breast cancer information and support: www.nci.nih.gov
- Breast implants: www.fda.gov/opacom/morechoices/breastim.html
- Breastfeeding: www.hhs.gov/hrsa/mchb
- Cancer information service: www.cancernet.nci.nih.gov
- Cerebral palsy: www.ninds.nih.gov
- Child abuse and neglect: www.acf.dhhs.gov/programs/cb
- Child care bureau: www.acf.dhhs.gov/programs/ccb
- Child health and development: www.nih.gov/nichd
- Child support enforcement: www.acf.dhhs.gov/programs/CSE
- Childhood immunization information: www.cdc.gov/nip
- Chronic diseases: www.cdc.gov/nccdphp
- Civil rights offices: www.hrsa.gov/oa.html
- Clinical practice guidelines: www.ahrq.gov/clinic/cpgsix.htm or www.ihs.gov/csp/customer.html
- Consumer affairs inquiries: www.ihs.gov/csp/customer.html
- Consumer complaint/fraud/referral help: www.hhs.gov/progorg/oig
- Consumer product safety hotline: www.cpsc.gov
- Cosmetics: www.vm.cfsan.fda.gov/~dms/cos-toc.html
- Deafness/speech/communication disorders: www.nih.gov/nidcd
- Dental/tooth decay: www.nidr.nih.gov
- Depression helpline: www.nimh.nih.gov
- Developmental disabilities: www.acf.dhhs.gov/programs/ADD
- Diabetes: www.niddk.nih.gov
- Digestive diseases: www.niddk.nih.gov
- Disabled infants: www.acf.dhhs.gov
- Disease prevention/health promotion: www.cdc.gov/nccdphp
- Drug/alcohol treatment referral: www.nida.nih.gov
- Drugs-adverse reactions: www.fda.gov/medwatch
- Drugs-prescription and OTC: www.fda.gov
- Drug use/adolescents: www.health.org or www.nida.hih.gov.html

- Eldercare: www.aoa.dhhs.gov/naic/ or www.aoa.dhhs.gov/elderpage.html
- Epilepsy: www.ninds.nih.gov
- Family planning: www.hhs.gov/progorg/opa
- Foster care: www.acf.dhhs.gov/programs/cb
- Fraud and abuse/Medicaid: www.hhs.gov/progorg/oig
- Food and Drug Administration: www.fda.gov/foi/foia2.htm
- Genome (Human) Research: www.nhgri.nih.gov
- Hazardous substances/Superfund sites: www.cdc.gov/niosh/homepage.html
- Headache: www.ninds.nih.gov
- Head injury: www.ninds.nih.gov
- Head Start: www.acf.dhhs.gov/programs/hsb
- Health care technology: www.ahrq.gov
- Health Info: www.hhs.gov
- Health maintenance organizations: www.hcfa.gov/medicare/mgdcar.htm
- Health professionals education: www.hrsa.dhhs.gov
- Herpes: www.niaid.nih.gov
- High blood pressure/cholesterol: www.nhlbi.nih.gov
- HIV/AIDS: www.hab.hrsa.gov
- Hospice: www.medicare.gov/publications.html
- Indian Health Service: www.ihs.gov
- HIS Publications: www.ihs.gov/PublicInfo/index.asp
- Infectious diseases: www.cdc.gov/ncidod.htm
- International and refugee health: www.cdc.gov
- Juvenile justice/delinquency information: www.ncjrs.org/ojjdp/juvoff ojjdp.html or www.fedstats.gov
- Kidney/urologic diseases: www.niddk.nih.gov
- Lead poisoning: www.hiehs.nih.gov
- Learning disabilities: www.ninds.nih.gov
- Leprosy (Hansen's disease): www.niaid.nih.gov
- Liver diseases: www.niddk.nih.gov
- Lung diseases: www.nhlbi.nih.gov
- Mammography: www.nci.nih.gov
- Medicaid/Medicare: www.hcfa.gov or www.hcfa.gov/medicaid/medicaid.htm
- Medicaid/Medicare fraud: www.hcfa.gov
- Medical devices: www.fda.gov/cdrh
- Medical school grants: www.hrsa.dhhs.gov
- Medicare (including Medigap): www.hcfa.gov
- Medicine, National Library of: www.nlm.nih.gov
- Mental health: www.samhsa.gov
- Mental retardation: www.acf.dhhs.gov/programs/pcmr
- Migrant worker health care: www.bphc.hrsa.dhhs.gov
- Missing children/runaways: www.missingkids.com
- National Health Service Corps: www.hrsa.dhhs.gov

- National Practitioner Data Bank: www.npdb-hipdb.com
- Nutrition: www.fns.usda.gov/fncs
- Occupational safety: www.osha.gov/index.html
- Organ and other transplantation: www.hrsa.dhhs.gov/osp
- Outcomes research: www.ahrq.gov
- Pain disorder/trauma helpline: www.ninds.nih.gov
- Paralysis/spinal cord injury: www.ninds.nih.gov
- Pregnancy/prenatal care/childbirth: www.hhs.gov/hrsa/mchb
- Pregnancy/substance abuse: www.cdc.gov/nccdphp/osh
- Radiological health: www.fda.gov/cdrh
- Radon safety helpline: www.ebtpages/airairporadon.html
- Rape Crisis Hotline: www.members.aol.com/NCMDR/index.html or www.bphc.hrsa.dhhs.gov/omwh/omwh_8.htm
- Refugee resettlement/immigration: www.acf.dhhs.gov/programs/orr
- Runaway youth/homelessness: www.nrscrisisline.org
- Rural health services: www.ruralhealth.hrsa.gov
- School health education: www.cdc.gov/nccdphp/dash/cshedef.htm
- Sexually transmitted disease Helpline: www.cdc.gov/nchstp/dstd/dstdp.html
- SIDS (sudden infant death syndrome): www.nichd.nih.gov
- National Cancer Institute: www.cancernet.nci.nih.gov
- Statistics: Health care and vital: www.ahrq.gov/data
- Stroke/neurological disorders: www.ninds.nih.gov
- Teen pregnancy: www.teenpregnancy.org or www.hrsa.dhhs.gov
- Toxic substances: www.niehs.nih.gov
- Travelers health information: www.cdc.gov/travel/index.htm
- Treatment/referral assistance: www.cdc.gov/travel/index.htm or www.ahrq.gov
- Uninsured assistance: www.hrsa.gov/cap/default.htm
- Urban Indian Health Programs: www.ihs.gov/Healthcare/general/programs.asp
- Vaccine adverse event to report: www.fda.gov/medwatch/ or www.fda.gov/cber
- Vaccine injury compensation: www.hrsa.dhhs.gov
- Veterinary medicine: www.fda.gov/cvm/default.htm
- Weight control/obesity information: www.niddk.nih.gov/health/nutrit.htm
- Welfare and AFDC jobs programs: www.acf.dhhs.gov/programs/cb
- Women's health: www.fda.gov/womens
- Women's health research: www.fda.gov/womens

Other Agencies

- Allergies/asthma: www.AAFA.org
- Alzheimer's disease: www.alzheimers.com
- Disabled children and youth: www.dredf.org
- Domestic violence: www.igc.org/fund/healthcare/res_center.htm

- Drug/alcohol—Information only: www.health.org
- Environmental health: www.neha.org
- Helene Fuld: www.fuld.org/welcome.htm
- Homelessness: www.prainc.com/nrc/info.htm
- Marrow donor program: www.marrow.org
- Osteoporosis: www.osteo.org
- Sickle cell disease: www.SickleCelldisease.org
- Smoking/tobacco: www.health.org
- Welfare information: www.welfareinfor.org
- Youth crisis hotline: www.nrscrisisline.org

Suggested Readings on Related Issues

The suggested readings are some resources for grant writing or ideas for future grants.

_____. 1999. Apolipoprotein E epsilon 4 allele (APOE epsilon 4) and Alzheimer's disease: Role of genetic testing for diagnosis and risk assessment. *Tecnologica MAP Supplements* 4–7.

Brakely, M.R. 1997. Tips for the novice grant-seeker: Implications for staff development specialists. *Journal of Staff Development* 13(3): 160–163.

Gaberson, K.B. 1997. What's the answer? What's the question? *Association of Operating Room Nurses Journal* 66(1): 148–151.

Kahn, C.R. 1994. Picking a research problem: The critical decision. *The New England Journal of Medicine* 330(21): 1530–1533.

Lorentzon, M. 1995. Multidisciplinary collaboration: Life line or drowning pool for nurse researchers? *Journal of Advanced Nursing* 22(5): 825–826.

Malone, R.E. 1996. Getting your study funded: Tips for new researchers. *Journal of Emergency Nursing* 22(5): 457–459.

Marshall, M.N., P.G. Shekelle, S. Leatherman, and R.H. Brook. 2000. Public disclosure of performance data: learning from the US experience. *Quality Health Care* 9(1): 53–7.

Patterson, E.R. and S. Bakewell-Sachs. 1998. Toward evidence based-practice. *Maternal Child Nursing (MCN)* 23: 278–280.

Ries, J.B. and C.G. Leukefeld. 1995. *Applying For Research Funding: Getting Started And Getting Funded*. London: Sage.

Sage, W.M. 1999. Regulating through information: disclosure laws and American health care. *Columbia Law Reviews* 99(7): 1701–829.

Triendl, R. 2000. World's academies seek a sustainable future [news]. *Nature* 405(6786): 501.

Van Dyke Hayes, K. 1999. Research grants and you: perfect together. *SCI Nursing* 17(3): 104–7.

Woolley, M. 1996. What are you waiting for? *Circulation* 94(8): 1802–1803.

Other Internet Resources

These resources are on the Internet. They represent tools for grant writing, statistical analyses, systematic reviews, or potential sources for project ideas. Included are literature search engines such as ERIC and Medline.

Systematic Reviews: For Evidence-Based Practice and Integrated Literature Reviews

- Cochrane Collaborative: www.hiru.mcmaster.ca/cochrane/centres/canadian/
- The Joanna Briggs Institute For Evidence Based Nursing and Midwifery: Systematic Reviews: www.joannabriggs.edu.au/sysmenu.html
- Systematic Reviews on Childhood Injury, Prevention and Interventions: www.depts.washington.edu/hiprc/childinjury/
- Thomas C. Chalmers Centre for Systematic Reviews: www.cheori.org/tcc/index.htm
- Vermont Oxford Network: www.vtoxford.org/

Grant Resources

- COS Funding Opportunities: Funded Research: www.fundedresearch.cos.com
- Department of Education Technology Innovation Challenge Grants: www.ed.gov/Technology/challenge
- Federal Government Grants, Loans and Financial Aid: www.americanfinancecenter.com
- Financial Aid Resource Center—Scholarships, Grants, Loans for College: www.theoldschool.org
- The Foundation Center: www.fdncenter.org
- Food: www.fda.gov
- Grants and Related Resources: www.lib.msu.edu/harris23/grants/federal.htm
- Grants Resources on the Internet: A Detailed Guide: www.library.wisc.edu/libraries/Memor
- Grants Web: www.infoserv.rttonet.psu.edu/gweb.htm
- HRSA Grants and Contracts: www.hrsa.dhhs.gov/grants.htm
- Internet Grateful Med V2.6: www.igm.nlm.nih.gov
- Justice Information Center (NCJRS): Justice Grants: www.ncjrs.org/fedgrant.htm
- Medline: Entrez-Pubmed: www.ncbi.nlm.nih.gov/PubMed
- NIH Center for Scientific Review Home Page: www.drg.nih.gov
- NIH Guide Index: www.med.nyu.edu/hih-guide.html
- NIH Office of Extramural Research-Grants: www.nih.gov/grants/oer.htm
- Office of Educational Technology: www.ed.gov/Technology
- Office of Science Grants and Contracts Web Site www.er.doe.gov/production/grants/grants
- Pell Grant Program: www.ed.gov/prog_info/SFA/StudentGuide/1998-9/pell.html

- The Grants Information Center: www.library.wisc.edu/libraries/Memor
- TRAM-Texas Research Administrators Group hosted by Arizona State University East. www.tram.east.asu.edu
- US Department of Education-Grants and Contracts: www.gcs.ed.gov
- Welcome to GrantsNet: www.grantsnet.org

Grant Writers/Reviewers

The Grant Doctors

PO Box 417212
Sacramento, CA 95841
Phone: (888) 208-2441
Fax: (800) 783-0238
E-mail: dave@thegrantdoctors.com
www.thegrantdoctors.com/

This is a for-profit group that provides grants consultants and proposal writers. Their mission is to provide the finest grants consulting service available.

Literature Searches

- Scientific Information: www.biolinks.com
- CINAHL Database: Cumulative Index to Nursing and Allied Health Literature: www.cihahl.com
- ERIC Database: Educational Research Information Collection: www.ericir.syr.edu/Cric
- Google: www.google.com
- Governmental Information: www.google.com/unclesam
- Legal Data: www.findlaw.com
- Medline Database: Search using either PubMed or Internet Grateful Med: www.nlm.nih.gov/databases/freemedl.html
- *Ingenta: The Global Research Gateway: www.ingenta.com/home/

Statistical Resources

Interactive Statistical Calculation Pages

This resource provides over 550 links to assist with statistical analyses: www.members.aol.com/johnp71/javastat.html

*This site is a portal to online information around the world. The center is in the United Kingdom, but they have merged with the Carl Organization that runs the Uncover and Reveal service from Denver, Colorado. These services assist researchers and educators set up delivery of literature reviews on a weekly basis or tables of contents for a designated number of journals for an annual subscription rate. The Carl Organization website is: www.carl.org

Power Analysis: Step by Step

An easy-to-follow format to estimate a power for the correct sample size: www.mp1-pwrc.usgs.gov/powcase/steps.html

Power Analysis Monitoring Programs: A Power Primer

This resource is just what it says a primer on the how to do a power calculation: www.mp1-pwrc.usgs.gov/powcase/primer.html

Power Calculator

With this resource, you choose a model and plug in information and out comes the power for a given sample: www.ebook.stat.ucla.edu/calculators/powercalc

Power Analysis of ANOVA Designs

This web site explains power calculations—what they are and how to do a power analysis: www.math.yorku.ca/SCS/Demos/power

SAS e-Intelligence

SAS software for power calculations and other statistical analyses: www.sas.com

Healthy People 2010 Goals and Objectives C

Healthy People 2010 is a national health promotion and disease prevention initiative. Its goals are to increase the quality and years of healthy life and eliminate health disparities. Grants that focus on health care practice, education, or research often require a clear tie to at least one goal and objective of this initiative.

Goals

1. Increase Quality and Years of Healthy Life
2. Eliminate Health Disparities

Objectives
Promote Health Behaviors

Physical Activity and Fitness

Goal: Improve the health, fitness, and quality of life of all Americans through the adoption and maintenance of regular, daily physical activity.

Objectives:

1. Leisure Time Physical Activity
   Example: Increase to 85 percent the proportion of people aged 18 and older who engage in any leisure time physical activity.
2. Sustained Physical Activity
3. Vigorous Physical Activity

*This list is a brief synopsis of the *Healthy People 2010* Goals and Objectives. One specific example is given for each category.

Source: Office of Disease Prevention and Health Promotion (2001). http://web.health.gov/healthypeople Washington DC.

4. Muscular Strength and Endurance
5. Flexibility
6. Vigorous Physical Activity, grades 9-12
7. Moderate Physical Activity, grades 9-12
8. Daily School Physical Education
9. Physical Education Requirement in Schools
10. School Physical Education Quality
11. Inclusion of Physical Activity in Health Education
12. Access to School Physical Activity Facilities
13. Worksite Physical Activity and Fitness
14. Clinician Counseling About Physical Activity

Nutrition

> **Goal: Promote health and reduce chronic disease risk, disease progression, debilitation, and premature death associated with dietary factors and nutritional status among all people of the United States.**

Objectives:

1. Healthy Weight
   Example: Increase to at least 60 percent the prevalence of healthy weight (defined as a BMI [Body Mass Index] equal to or greater than 19.0 and less than 25.0) among all people aged 20 and older.
2. Obesity in adults
3. Overweight and Obesity in Children/Adolescents
4. Growth Retardation
5. Fat Intake
6. Saturated Fat Intake
7. Vegetable and Fruit Intake
8. Vegetable and Fruit Intake
9. Grain Product Intake
10. Calcium Intake
11. Sodium Intake
12. Iron Deficiency
13. Anemia in Pregnant Women
14. Meals and Snacks at School
15. Nutrition Education, Elementary Schools
16. Nutrition Education, Middle/Junior High Schools
17. Nutrition Education, Senior High Schools
18. Nutrition Assessment and Planning
19. Nutrition Counseling
20. Food Security

Tobacco Use

Goal: Reduce disease, disability, and death related to tobacco use and exposure to secondhand smoke by (1) preventing initiation of tobacco use, (2) promoting cessation of tobacco use, (3) reducing exposure to secondhand smoke, and (4) changing social norms and environments that support tobacco use.

Objectives:

1. Adult Tobacco Use
   Example: Reduce to 13 percent the proportion of adults (18 and older) who use tobacco products.
2. Cigarette Smoking During Pregnancy
3. Adolescent Tobacco Use
4. Age at First Use of Tobacco
5. Adolescent Never Smokers
6. Smoking Cessation
7. Smoking Cessation During Pregnancy
8. Smoking Cessation By New Mothers
9. Smoking Cessation Attempts Among Adolescents
10. Advice to Quit Smoking
11. Treatment of Nicotine Addiction
12. Providers Advising Smoking Cessation
13. Physician Inquires About Secondhand Smoke
14. Tobacco-Free Schools
15. Worksite Smoking Policies
16. Smoke-Free Air Laws
17. Enforcement of Minors' Access Laws
18. Retail License Suspension for Sales to Minors
19. Adolescent Disapproval of Smoking
20. Adolescent Perception of Harm of Tobacco Use
21. Tobacco Use Prevention Education
22. Cigarette Price Increase
23. Tobacco Product Price Increase
24. State Tobacco Control Programs
25. Preemptive Tobacco Control Laws

Promote Health and Safe Communities

Educational and Community-Based Programs

Goal: Increase the quality, availability, and effectiveness of educational and community-based programs designed to prevent disease and improve the health and quality of life of the American people.

Objectives:

1. High School Completion
   Example: Increase the high school completion rate to at least 90 percent.
2. School Health Education
3. Undergraduate Health Risk Behavior Information
4. School Nurse-to-Student Ratio
5. Worksite Health Promotion Programs
6. Participation in Employer-Sponsored Health Promotion Activities
7. Patient Satisfaction with Health Care Provider Communication
8. Patient and Family Education
9. Community Disease Prevention and Health Promotion Activities
10. Community Health Promotion Initiatives
11. Culturally Appropriate Community Health Promotion Programs
12. Elderly Participation in Community Health Promotion

Environmental Health

Goal: Health for all through a healthy environment.

Objectives:

1. Air Quality
   Example: The air will be safer to breathe for 100 percent of the people living in areas that exceed all National Ambient Air Quality Standards (NAAQS).
2. Emission Reduction
3. Cleaner Alternative Fuels
4. Waterborne Disease
5. Water-Related Adverse Health Effects
6. Surface Water Health Risks
7. Beach Closings
8. Discharge from Livestock Production Operations
9. Watersheds with Contaminant Problems
10. Poisonings from Contaminated Fish
11. Blood Lead Levels
12. Risks to Human Health and Environment by Hazardous Waste Sites
13. Pesticide Poisonings
14. Energy Recovery
15. Municipal Solid Waste
16. Exposure to Tobacco Smoke
17. Testing for Lead-Based Paint
18. Exposure to Household Hazardous Chemicals
19. Household Levels of Lead Dust and Allergens
20. Carbon Monoxide Poisonings
21. Radon Testing

22. Exposure to Household Chemicals
23. Exposure to Persistent Chemicals
24. Monitoring of Exposure to Selected Chemicals
25. Environmental and Environmental Health Information Systems
26. Monitoring Diseases Caused by Environmental Hazards
27. Global Burden of Disease
28. Infectious and Parasitic Diseases
29. Consultation on Environmental Issues
30. Tracking Mechanism of Exported Pesticides
31. Diseases Among U.S. Travelers Overseas
32. Total Pesticide Exposure
33. Uniform International Guidelines for Environmental Quality

Food Safety

Goal: Reduce the number of foodborne illnesses.

Objectives:

1. Foodborne Infections
   Example: Reduce, by 50 percent for bacteria and 10 percent for parasites, the proportion of infections caused by key foodborne pathogens.
2. Salmonella and Escherichia Coli
3. Listeria Monocytogenes and Vibrio Vulnificus
4. Antimicrobial-Resistant Bacterial Pathogens
5. Food-Induced Anaphylaxis
6. Food Handling by Consumers
7. Food Handling in Retail Establishments
8. Pesticide Residue Tolerances
9. Limits for Mycotoxins

Injury/Violence Prevention

Goal: Reduce the incidence and severity of injuries from unintentional causes, as well as violence and abuse.

Objectives:

Injuries that Cut Across Intent

1. Nonfatal head injuries
   Example: Reduce nonfatal head injuries so that hospitalizations for this condition are no more than 74 per 100,000 people.
2. Nonfatal spinal cord injuries
3. Firearm-Related Deaths
4. Homes with Firearms
5. Laws Requiring Proper Firearm Storage

6. Child Death Review Systems
7. Injury Prevention and Safety Education

Unintentional Injuries

8. Deaths from Unintentional Injuries
9. Emergency Department Visits
10. Nonfatal Unintentional Injuries
11. Motor Vehicle Crashes
12. Pedestrian Deaths
13. Nonfatal Motor Vehicle Injuries
14. Pedestrian Injuries
15. Safety Belts and Child Restraints
16. Primary Enforcement Laws for Safety Belt Use
17. Use of Motorcycle Helmets
18. Motorcycle Helmet Laws
19. Graduated Driver Licensing
20. Residential Fire Deaths
21. Smoke Alarms
22. Deaths form Falls
23. Hip Fractures
24. Drowning Deaths
25. Bicycle Helmet Laws
26. Bicycle Helmet Use, High School Students
27. Bicycle Helmet Use
28. Nonfatal Poisoning
29. Deaths from Unintentional Poisoning
30. Nonfatal Dog Bite Injuries
31. Head, Face, Eye, and Mouth Protection in school Sports
32. Injury Prevention Counseling

Violence and Abusive

33. Homicides
34. Maltreatment of Children
35. Physical Abuse by Intimate Partners
36. Forced Sexual Intercourse
37. Emergency Housing for Battered Women
38. Sexual Assault Other Than Rape
39. Physical Assaults
40. Physical Fighting Among Adolescents
41. Weapon Carrying by Adolescents

Occupational Safety and Health

Goal: Promote worker health and safety through prevention.

Objectives:

1. Deaths from Work-Related Injuries
   Example: Reduce deaths from work-related injuries to no more than 3.6 per 100,000 workers.
2. Work-Related Injuries
3. Workplace Injury and Illness Surveillance
4. Overexertion or Repetitive Motion
5. Pneumoconiosis Deaths
6. Work-Related Homicides
7. Workplace Assaults
8. Noise-Induced Permanent Threshold Shift
9. Blood Lead Levels Greater than 25 g/dL
10. Blood Lead Levels Greater than 10 g/dL
11. Occupational Skin Diseases/Disorders
12. Latex Allergy
13. Tractor Rollover Protection Systems
14. Worksite Stress Reduction Programs
15. Hepatitis B Infections
16. Hepatitis B Vaccinations

Oral Health

Goal: Improve the health and quality of life for individuals and communities by preventing and controlling oral, dental, and craniofacial diseases, conditions, and injuries and improving access to oral health care for all.

Objectives:

1. Caries Experience
   Example: Reduce dental caries (cavities) in primary and permanent teeth (mixed dentition) so that the proportion of children who have had one or more cavities (filled or unfilled) is no more than 15 percent among children aged 2-4, 40 percent among children aged 6-8, and 55 percent among adolescents aged 15.
2. Untreated Dental Decay
3. Root Caries
4. No Tooth Loss
5. Complete Tooth Loss
6. Gingivitis
7. Periodontal Disease
8. Stage I Oropharyngeal Cancer Lesions
9. Dental Sealants
10. Water Fluoridation
11. Topical Fluorides

12. Screening/Counseling for 2-year-olds
13. Screening, Referral, Treatment for First-Time School Program Children
14. Adult Use of Oral Health Care System
15. School-Based Health Centers with Oral Health Component
16. Community Health Centers with Direct Oral Health Service Component
17. Exams and Services for Those in Long-Term Care Facilities
18. Referral for Cleft Lip/Palate
19. State-Based Surveillance System
20. State and Local Dental Programs
21. Screening for Oropharyngeal Cancer

Improve Systems for Personal and Public Health Access To Quality Health Services

Goal: Improve access to comprehensive, high quality health care across a continuum of care.

Clinical Prevention Services

Objectives:

A.1 Uninsured children and adults
Example: Reduce to 0 percent the proportion of children and adults under 65 without health care coverage.
A 2 Insurance Coverage
A 3 Routine Screening About Lifestyle Risk Factors
A 4 Reporting on Service Delivery
A 5 Training to Address Health Disparities

Primary Care

B 1 Source of Ongoing Primary Care
B 2 Failure to Obtain All Needed Health Care
B 3 Lack of Primary Care Visits
B 4 Access to Primary Care Providers in Underserved Areas
B 5 Racial/Ethnic Minority Representation in the Health Professions
B 6 Preventable Hospitalization Rates for Chronic Illness

Emergency Services

C 1 Access to Emergency Medical Services
C 2 Insurance Coverage
C 3 Toll-Free Poison Control Center Number
C 4 Time-Dependent Care for Cardiac Symptoms
C 5 Special Needs of Children
C 6 Follow-up Mental Health Services

Long-Term Care and Rehabilitative Services

D 1 Functional Assessments
D 2 Primary Care Evaluation

D 3 Access to the Continuum of Services
D 4 Pressure Ulcers

Family Planning

Goal: Every pregnancy in the United States should be intended.

Objectives:

1. Planned pregnancy.
   Example: Increase to at least 70 percent the proportion of all pregnancies among women aged 15-44 that are planned (i.e., intended).
2. Repeat Unintended Births.
3. Contraceptive Use, Females.
4. Contraceptive Failure.
5. Postcoital Hormonal Contraception.
6. Male Involvement in Family Planning.
7. Adolescent Pregnancy.
8. Sexual Intercourse Before Age 15.
9. Adolescent Sexual Intercourse.
10. Pregnancy and STD Preventive Methods.
11. Pregnancy Prevention Education.
12. School Requirement for Classes on Human Sexuality, Pregnancy Prevention, etc.
13. Impaired Fecundity.

Maternal, Infant, and Child Health

Goal: Improve maternal health and pregnancy outcomes and reduce rates of disability in infants, thereby improving the health and well-being of women, infants, children, and families in the United States. The health of a population is reflected in the health of its most vulnerable members. A major focus of many public health efforts, therefore, is improving the health of pregnant women and their infants, including reductions in rates of birth defects, risk factors for infant death, and deaths of infants and their mothers.

Objectives:

1. Infant Mortality
   Example: Reduce the infant mortality rate to no more than 5 per 1,000 live births.
2. Infant Mortality from Birth Defects
3. SIDS Mortality
4. Child Mortality
5. Fetal Death
6. Perinatal Mortality

7. Maternal Mortality
8. Maternal Morbidity
9. Preconception Counseling
10. Prenatal Care
11. Quality of Prenatal Care
12. Serious Developmental Disabilities
13. Childbirth Classes
14. Postpartum Visits
15. Very Low Birthweight Babies Born at Level III Hospitals
16. Cesarean Delivery
17. Low Birthweight
18. Preterm Birth
19. Weight Gain During Pregnancy
20. Infant Sleep Position
21. Alcohol Use During Pregnancy
22. Tobacco Use During Pregnancy
23. Drug Use During Pregnancy
24. Fetal Alcohol Syndrome
25. Prenatal Exposure to Teratogenic Prescription Medication
26. Neural Tube Defects
27. Folic Acid Intake
28. Folate Level
29. Breastfeeding
30. Exclusive Breastfeeding
31. Newborn Screening
32. Sepsis Among Infants with Sickling Hemoglobinopathies
33. Newborn Hearing Screening
34. Training in Genetic Testing
35. Understanding of Inherited Sensitivities to Disease
36. Genetic Testing
37. Primary Care Services for Babies 18 months and Younger
38. Screening for Vision, Hearing, Speech, and Language Impairments
39. Service Systems for Children with Chronic and Disabling Conditions

Medical Product Safety

Goal: Ensure the safest and most effective possible use of medical products.

Objectives:

1. Monitoring of Adverse Drug Reactions
   Example: By the year 2010, compatible with a requirement to protect the privacy of each individual, there will be a population base of 20,000,000

individuals under close electronically monitored safety surveillance for indicators of adverse events associated with medical therapies.

2. Approval of Medical Products
3. Response form Managed Care Organizations Regarding Adverse Drug Reactions
4. Linked Automated Information Systems
5. Drug Alert Systems
6. Provider Review of Medications Taken by Patients
7. Complementary and Alternative Health Care
8. Safety-Related Labeling Changes
9. Updates to Drug Alert Systems
10. Patient Information About Prescriptions

Public Health Infrastructure

Goal: Ensure that the public health infrastructure at the Federal, State, and local levels has the capacity to provide essential public health services.

Objectives:

1. Competencies for Public Health Workers
   Example: Increase the number of States and local jurisdictions that incorporate specific competencies for public health workers into their public health personnel system.
2. Training in Essential Public Health Services
3. Continuing Education and Training by Public Health Agencies
4. Use of Standard Occupational Classification System
5. Onsite Access to Data
6. Access to Public Health Information and Surveillance Data
7. Tracking Healthy People 2010 Objectives for Select Populations
8. Data Collection for Healthy People 2010 Objectives
9. Use of Geocoding in Health Data Systems
10. Performance Standards for Essential Public Health Services
11. Health Improvement Plans
12. Access to Laboratory Services
13. Access to Comprehensive Epidemiology Services
14. Model Statues Related to Essential Public Health Services
15. Data on Public Health Expenditures
16. Collaboration and Cooperation in Prevention Research Efforts
17. Summary Measures of Population Health and the Public Health Infrastructure

Health Communication

Goal: Improve the quality of health-related decisions through effective communication.

Objectives:

1. Public Access to Health Information
   Example: Increase to percent the proportion of cities and counties that have a publicly or privately funded program or activity to promote and enhance public access to health information for underserved populations.
2. Centers for Excellence
3. Evaluation of Communication Programs
4. Satisfaction with Health Information
5. Health Literacy Programs
6. Quality of Health Information
7. Health Communication/Media Technology Curricula

Prevent and Reduce Diseases and Disorders
Arthritis, Osteoporosis, and Chronic Back Conditions

Goal: Reduce the impact of several major musculoskeletal conditions by reducing the occurrence, impairment, functional limitation, and limitation, and limitation in social participation (i.e., disability) due to arthritis and other rheumatic conditions; reducing the prevalence of osteoporosis and resulting fractures by increasing reducing activity limitation due to chronic back conditions.

Objectives:

Arthritis

1. Mean Days Without Severe Pain
   Example: Increase mean days without severe pain for U.S. adults with arthritis to more than 20 of the past 30 days.
2. Activity Limitations
3. Personal Care Limitations
4. Help in Coping
5. Labor Force Participation
6. Racial Differences in Total Knee Replacement Rate
7. Failure to See a Doctor for Arthritis
8. Early Diagnosis and Treatment of Systemic Rheumatic Diseases
9. Arthritis Education Among Patients
10. Provision of Arthritis Education
11. Dietary Practices and Physical Activity

Osteoporosis

12. Prevalence
13. Counseling about Prevention, 13 and over
14. Counseling about Prevention, Women 50 and Over

Chronic Back Conditions

15. Activity Limitations

Cancer

Goal: Reduce the burden of cancer on the U.S. population by decreasing cancer incidence, morbidity, and mortality rates.

Objectives:

1. Cancer Deaths
   Example: Reduce cancer deaths to a rate of no more than 103 per 100,000 people.
2. Lung Cancer Deaths
3. Breast Cancer Deaths
4. Cervical Cancer Deaths
5. Colorectal Cancer Deaths
6. Oropharyngeal Cancer Deaths
7. Prostate Cancer Deaths
8. Sun Exposure
9. Provider Counseling About Preventive Measures
10. Pap Tests
11. Colorectal Screening Examination
12. Oral, Skin, and Digital Rectal Examinations
13. Breast Examination and Mammogram
14. Physician Counseling of High-Risk Patients
15. Statewide Cancer Registries
16. Cancer Survival Rates

Diabetes

Goal: Reduce needless disease and economic burden for all persons with, or at risk for, diabetes mellitus.

Objectives:

1. Type 2 Diabetes
   Example: Decrease the incidence of Type 2 diabetes to 2.5 per 1,000 persons per year.
2. Diabetes Prevalence

3. Diagnosis of Diabetes
4. Diabetes-Related Deaths
5. Diabetes-Related Deaths Among Known Persons with Diabetes
6. Cardiovascular Deaths
7. Perinatal Mortality in Infants of Mothers with Diabetes
8. Congenital Malformations in Infants or Mothers with Diabetes
9. Foot Ulcers
10. Lower Extremity Amputations
11. Visual Impairment
12. Blindness
13. Proteinuria
14. End-Stage Renal Disease
15. Lipid Assessment
16. Glycosylated Hemoglobin Measurement
17. Urinary Measurement of Microalbumin
18. Controlled Blood Pressure
19. Dilated Eye Examinations
20. Foot Examinations
21. Aspirin Therapy
22. Self-Blood Glucose Monitoring
23. Diabetes Education

Disability and Secondary Conditions

Goal: Promote health and prevent secondary conditions among persons with disabilities, including eliminating disparities between person with disabilities and the U.S. population.

Objectives:

1. Core Data Sets
   Example: Include a comparable core set of items to identify "people with disabilities" in all data sets used for Healthy People 2010.
2. Depression
3. Days of Anxiety
4. Healthy Days Among Adults with Activity Limitations Who Need Assistance
5. Personal and Emotional Support
6. Satisfaction with Life.
7. Print Size on Medicine, Patient Instructional Materials, and Syringe Markings
8. Employment Rates
9. Inclusion of Children with Disabilities in Regular Education Programs
10. Compliance with Americans with Disabilities Act
11. Environmental Barriers
12. Disability Surveillance and Health Promotion Programs

Heart Disease and Stroke

Goal: Enhance the cardiovascular health and quality of life of all Americans through improvement of medical management, prevention and control of risk factors, and promotion of healthy lifestyle behaviors.

Objectives:

1. Coronary Heart Disease Deaths
   Example: Reduce coronary heart disease deaths to no more than 51 per 100,000 population.
2. Female Deaths After Heart Attack
3. Knowledge of Early Warning Symptoms of Heart Attack
4. Provider Counseling About Early Warning Symptoms of Heart Attack
5. Females Aware of Heart Disease as the Leading Cause of Death
6. High Blood Pressure
7. Controlled High Blood Pressure
8. Action to Help Control Blood Pressure
9. Blood Pressure Monitoring
10. Serum Cholesterol Levels
11. Blood Cholesterol Levels
12. Blood Cholesterol Screening
13. Treatment of LDL Cholesterol
14. Stroke Deaths
15. Knowledge of Early Warning Symptoms of Stroke
16. Provider Counseling About Early Warning Symptoms of Stroke

HIV

Goals: Prevent HIV transmission and associated morbidity and mortality by (1) ensuring that all persons at risk for HIV infection know their sero-status, (2) ensuring that those person not infected with HIV remain un-infected, (3) ensuring that those person infected with HIV do not transmit HIV to others, and (4) ensuring that those infected with HIV are accessing the most effective therapies possible.

Objectives:

1. AIDS Incidence
   Example: Confine annual incidence of diagnosed AIDS cases among adolescents and adults to nor more than 12 per 100,000 population.
2. HIV Incidence
3. Condom Use
4. Screening for STDs and Immunization for Hepatitis B
5. HIV Counseling and Testing for Injecting Drug Users
6. HIV Counseling and Testing for Prison Inmates

7. Knowledge of HIV Serostatus Among People with Tuberculosis
8. Classroom Education on HIV and STDs
9. Compliance with Public Health Service Treatment Guidelines
10. Mortality Due to HIV Infection
11. Years of Healthy Life Following HIV Diagnosis
12. Perinatally Acquired HIV Infection
13. Treatment for Injecting Drug Use

Immunization and Infectious Diseases

Goal: Prevent disease, disability, and death from infectious disease, including vaccine-preventable diseases.

Objectives:

1. Vaccine-Preventable Diseases
   Example: Reduce indigenous cases of vaccine-preventable disease.
2. Impact of Influenza Vaccinations
3. Hepatitis A
4. Hepatitis B in Infants
5. Hepatitis B, under 25
6. Hepatitis B in Adults
7. Deaths form Hepatitis B-Related Cirrhosis and Liver Cancer
8. Hepatitis C
9. Identification of Persons with Chronic Hepatitis C
10. Deaths from Hepatitis C-Related Cirrhosis and Liver Cancer
11. Tuberculosis
12. Hospital-Acquired Infections
13. Hospital-Acquired Infections form Antimicrobial-Resistant Microorganisms
14. Antimicrobial use in Intensive Care
15. Occupational Needle-Stick Exposure
16. Bacterial Meningitis
17. Invasive Pneumococcal Infections
18. Invasive Early-Onset Group B Streptococcal Disease
19. Lyme Disease
20. Peptic Ulcer Hospitalizations
21. Immunization of Children 19-35 Months
22. States with 90 percent Immunization Coverage
23. Immunization Coverage for Children in Day Care, Kindergarten, and First Grade
24. Immunizations Among Adults
25. Curative Therapy for Tuberculosis
26. Preventive Therapy Among High-Risk Persons with Tuberculosis

27. Antibiotics for Ear Infections
28. Antibiotics Prescribed for Colds
29. Inappropriate Rabies Post-exposure Prophylaxis
30. 2-year-olds Receiving Vaccinations as Part of Primary Care
31. Provider Measurement of Immunization Coverage Levels
32. Immunization Registries
33. Vaccine-Associated Adverse Reactions
34. Febrile Seizures Caused by Pertussis Vaccines
35. Preventions Services for International Travelers
36. Laboratory Confirmation of Tuberculosis Cases

Mental Health and Mental Disorders

Goal: Improve the mental health of all Americans by ensuring appropriate, high-quality services informed by scientific research.

Objectives:

1. Suicide
   Example: Reduce suicides to no more than 9.6 per 100,000 people.
2. Injurious Suicide Attempts
3. Unipolar Major Depression
4. Mental Disorders Among Children and Adolescents
5. Serious Mental Illness Among Homeless People
6. Employment of Persons with Serious Mental Disorders
7. Disabilities Associated with Mental Disorders
8. Mental Health Services for People with Mental and Emotional Problems
9. Culturally Competent Mental Health Services
10. Provider Training in Screening for Mental Health Problems in Children
11. Provider Training in Addressing Mental Health Problems in Children
12. Provider Review of Patients' Cognitive, Emotional, and Behavioral Functioning
13. Primary Care Provider Assessment of Mental Health of Children
14. Mental Health Benefits
15. Access to Mental Benefits
16. Children's Access to Mental Health Services
17. Comparability of Mental Health Insurance
18. Children with Mental Health Insurance
19. Jail Diversion for Serious Mentally Ill Adults
20. Mental Health Screening by Juvenile Justice Facilities
21. Crisis and Ongoing Mental Health Services for the Elderly
22. State Plans to Address Co-occurring Disorders
23. Consumer Satisfaction With Services
24. Offices of Consumer Affairs of Mental Health Services

Respiratory Diseases

Goal: Raise the public's awareness of the signs and symptoms of lung diseases and what to do when they experience them—specifically symptoms of asthma, chronic obstructive pulmonary disease (COPD), and obstructive sleep apnea, and promote lung health through better detection, treatment, and education.

Objectives:

Asthma

1. Deaths
   Example: Reduce asthma death rate to no more than 14 per million population.
2. Hospitalizations
3. Emergency Department Visits
4. Activity Limitations
5. School or Work Days Lost
6. Patient Education
7. Continuing Medical Education
8. Written Asthma Management Plans
9. Counseling on Early Signs of Worsening Asthma
10. Instruction on Peak Expiratory Flow Monitoring
11. Short-Acting Inhaled Beta Agonists
12. Long-Term Management
13. Surveillance System

Chronic Obstructive Pulmonary Disease

14. Prevalence
15. Deaths
16. Culturally Competent Care
17. Training in Early Signs of COPD

Obstructive Sleep Apnea

18. Medical Evaluation
19. Follow-up Medical Care
20. Vehicular Accidents
21. Training in Sleep Medicine

Sexually Transmitted Diseases

Goal: A society where healthy sexual relationships, free of infection as well as coercion and unintended pregnancy, are the norms.

Objectives:

1. Chlamydia
   Example: Reduce the prevalence of Chlamydia tracheomatis infections among young person (15 to 24 years old) to no more than 3.0 percent.

2. Gonorrhea
3. Primary and Secondary Syphilis
4. Herpes Simplex Virus Type 2 Infection
5. Human Papilloma Virus Infection
6. Pelvic Inflammatory Disease
7. Fertility Problems
8. Congenital Syphilis
9. Neonatal STDs
10. Heterosexually Transmitted HIV
11. STD Clinics
12. School-Based Services
13. Medicaid Contracts
14. Reimbursement for Treatment of Partners of STD Patients
15. Training in STD-Related Services
16. Television Messages
17. Screening for Genital Chlamydia
18. Screening of Pregnant Women
19. Screening in Youth Detention Facilities and Jails
20. Compliance with CDC Guidelines for Treatment of STDs
21. Provider Referral Services for Sexual Partners
22. Reimbursement for Counseling on Reproductive Health Issues
23. Provider Counseling during initial Visits

Substance Abuse

Goal: Reduce substance abuse and thereby protect the health, safety, and quality of life of all Americans, especially the Nation's children.

Objectives:

1. Motor Vehicle Crashes
   Example: Reduce deaths and injuries caused by alcohol and drug-related motor vehicle crashes.
2. Cirrhosis Deaths
3. Drug-Related Deaths
4. Drug Abuse-Related Emergency Department Visits
5. Drug-Free Youth
6. Adolescent Use of Illicit Substances
7. Binge Drinking
8. Riding with a Driver Who Has Been Drinking
9. Alcohol Consumption
10. Steroid Use
11. Inhalant Use
12. Alcohol and Drug-Related Violence

13. Alcohol-Related Drowning
14. Peer Disapproval of Substance Abuse
15. Perception of Risk Associated with Substance Abuse
16. Treatment Gap for Illicit Drugs
17. Treatment Gap for Problem Alcohol Use
18. Services for School-Aged Children
19. Screening and Treatment of Patients 60 and Older
20. Lost Productivity
21. Community Partnerships and Coalitions
22. Administrative License Revocation Laws
23. Blood Alcohol Concentration Levels

Sample Forms and Other Documents D

Grants require several fairly standard forms and documents. This appendix gives examples of the following:

- Letter of intent
- Concept paper
- Abstract
- Research plan
- Protocol worksheet
- PH398 forms, including: face sheet, budget page (total), budget justification, biosketch (biographical sketch), and grant checklist.
- Pink Sheet
- Grant Application Process Planning Tool (GAPPT)

The first is the letter of intent to be sent to indicate to a funding agency that you plan on submitting a grant. The next form is the concept paper, which briefly describes the project to a funding agency. The abstract gives a very brief sketch of the project. The research plan is the brief outline of the step-by-step project blueprint. The protocol worksheet is an example of a form that a researcher can follow to make sure that the intervention steps are carried out appropriately.

The next set of forms consists of some of the forms required by the Public Health 398 NIH research or training grants. Included is a face sheet, budget page, budget justification form, biosketch, and grant checklist.

The Pink Sheet is the funding agency's grant critique. The final document is a Grant Application Process Planning Tool (GAPPT) that gives a suggested timeline for grant writing.

Letter of Intent

January 23, 2001
Applications Officer
March of Dimes Birth Defects Foundation
Greater Cincinnati Chapter
Cincinnati, Ohio

RE: Call for Educational Grants

Dear Grant Applications Officer:

As a practicing nurse and educator I am seeing an increasing number of infants born alcohol exposed. Yet, in our prenatal clinics the report rates average about 2 percent. We have found that some perinatal health professionals still advocate use of alcohol to women during the last trimester if the fetus is too active. Having completed substance abuse training through NIAAA I know the dangers of this practice.

I am submitting a grant to the CDC for Fetal Alcohol Syndrome Prevention. As a corollary part to this project, I want to provide education to the health professionals in eight perinatal clinics in Cincinnati. My research team and I believe that with education we can heighten the awareness and increase the number of women identified during pregnancy that use alcohol. It is our hope that such education will result in a decreased incidence of Fetal Alcohol Syndrome. This proposed project fits well with your mission to decrease birth defects and increase awareness of potential perinatal problems that result in birth defects. I would like to submit this proposal for your next funding cycle.

Thank you in advance for your consideration of this proposed project. We look forward to hearing from you.

Sincerely,

Carole Kenner, DNS, RNC, FAAN
Professor of Clinical Nursing, University of Illinois at Chicago

Concept Paper

January 23, 2001
Agency for Healthcare Research and Quality
2101 E. Jefferson Street, Suite 501
Rockville, MD 20852

RE: Call for Health Care Policy Research

Dear Applications Officer:

As a neonatal nurse and an educator I have become increasing aware of the need for health policy research in the area of Last Precepts and End-of-Life Care in the newborn/infant population. Attached you will find the concept paper outlining this issue.

Concept Paper

Background/Significance

Low-birthweight infants (under 5.5 pounds) remain a problem in the U.S. despite educational efforts to promote good prenatal care. Since 1984 the incidence of low-birthweight births has increased to the present level of 7.5 per 1,000 live births. This steady rise contributes to the increase in mortality rate during the first month of life. Notably, 2/3s of all infant deaths are neonatal (first 28 days of life) death (http://www.childstats.gov). Morbidity and mortality are only part of the issue. Questions are being raised about what health care professionals are doing to assist the child who is dying and his/her family. The answer is little in terms of palliative or hospice care for the newborn and infant populations. Most of the emphasis of end-of-life care and last precepts centers on the child with cancer or adult health care issues. Little health policy reflects the younger population.

Palliative care is a "philosophy of care that provides a combination of active and compassionate therapies intended to comfort and support patients and families who are living with life-threatening illness, while being sensitive and respectful of their religious, cultural, and personal beliefs, values, and traditions" (Canadian Palliative Care Association, 1995). End-of-Life (EOL) Care encompasses palliative care. EOL refers to care for the terminally ill who are not likely to survive.

In December, 1997, the Task Force on Palliative Care developed the *Last acts, Care and caring for the end of life precepts of palliative Care.* To date more than 30 professional associations have endorsed these precepts, few are child oriented. The precepts are broad and need to be translated to fit the child and family model of care. To this end professional organizations were brought together by Johns Hopkins to work on this national problem, EOL across the lifespan. Leaders from 22 national nursing organization representing 463,000 nurses met in September, 2000 in Baltimore to attend the Nursing Leadership Academy in End-of-Life Care. This Academy was funded by a grant from the Open Society Institute's Project on Death in America. Following this meeting the charge was given to participants to work with like associations to gain strength in numbers to adapt the Last Precepts to their population. The National Association of Neonatal Nurses (NANN), Society of Pediatric Nurses (SPN), and Association of Pediatric Oncology Nurses (APON) joined to work towards this goal.

Conceptual Model

Dame Cicely Saunder's developed a Model of Whole Person Suffering (Krammer, Muri, Gooding-Kellar, Williams, & von Gunten, 1999). The model considers 4 aspects: physical, psychological, spiritual, and social. The emphasis is on maximizing quality of life and function and not the medical model of cure. This model requires a collaborative approach to care with all health care professions represented. One difficulty in implementing this model is the push for cost containment in health care delivery. Ethical challenges arise from the desire to provide EOL care and the need for cost containment measures.

Working with newborns and infants the family is the unit of care just as Saunder's model suggests (Krammer, Ring, Martinex, Jacobs, and Williams, 2001).

Health Policy Implications and Projected Research

To date there is little support by Medicaid for EOL care. Health care policies need to be changed to include EOL benefits. The nurse coordinates care as a family prepares for discharge. For the newborn or infant who is dying there are few options if the family cannot pay. This situation must be changed. The magnitude of this problem is not well defined so the first step is to conduct a pilot study to determine the number of children and their families who require hospice or palliative care, who are Medicaid eligible but who cannot received support for these services. This pilot will be conducted as a prospective study of families discharged from The Children's Hospital since 1999 to present and whose child is still alive but would benefit from hospice or palliative care. Concurrently the researchers will conduct a national survey of legislators to determine if they support inclusion of such care under Medicaid benefits-why or why not. This research is to determine the barriers to changing health policy. The final step in the research is to formulate policy based on the preliminary findings that will then be tested in the full research study. The project's timeline is one year.

References

Canadian Palliative Care Association (1995). *Canadian palliative care association: Palliative care: Towards a consensus in standardized principles of practice.* Ontario, Canada.

Krammer, L.M., Muir, J.C., Gooding-Kellar, N., Williams, M.B., and von Gunten, C. F. 1999. Palliative care and oncology: Opportunities for oncology nursing. *Oncology Nursing Updates* 6: 1–12.

Krammer, L.M., Ring, A.A., Martinex, J., Jacobs, M.J., & Williams, M.B., (2001). The nurse's role in interdisciplinary and palliative care. In M.L. Matzo and D.W. Sherman (eds.). *Palliative Care Nursing: Quality Care to the End of Life.* New York: Springer, pp. 118–139.

Note: This concept paper is fabricated. It would need many more details in terms of statistics and more details about the project than space will allow. If the legislators were truly to be polled a representation of some current policies that either support or refute Medicaid benefits should be included. A very defined target for the study would include hospital data, statistics of the surrounding area, and state statistics.

Abstract

Purpose: To identify physiologic and behavioral responses of extremely preterm infants to a routinely administered painful stimulus (heelstick for necessary blood sampling) and to determine how postconceptional age (PCA) may influence pain responses.

Subjects: Nonprobability convenience sample of 11 preterm infants born at 24-26 weeks PCA

Design: Quasi-experimental, repeated measures design

Methods: The Neonatal Individualized Developmental Care Assessment Program (NIDCAP) method was used to assess infant responses prior to, during, and following a heelstick procedure performed at weekly intervals between ages 27-32 weeks PCA.

Main Outcome Measures: Univariate indicators of pain including physiologic (heart rate, oxygen saturation, and respiratory rate) and behavioral (brow bulge, eye squeeze, and 45 NIDCAP variables) responses were examined. Additionally, the Premature Infant Pain Profile (PIPP) was used as a composite measure to assess pain.

Principal Results: Heart rate increased while oxygen saturation and respiratory rate decreased during the most invasive phase (stick/squeeze) of the procedure for infants between 27-32 weeks PCA. Increased PIPP scores and increased percent of occurrence of brow bulge and eye squeeze were also noted during the stick/squeeze phase. Although trends were noted towards increased behavioral stress between baseline and stick/squeeze values, these behaviors were not statistically significant across phases of the heelstick procedure. Finger splay increased significantly in magnitude of occurrence between 27 and 32 weeks PCA, while other NIDCAP variables, physiologic measures, facial variables and PIPP scores were not sensitive to differences in PCA.

Conclusions: Former 24-26 week preterm infants who are between 27 and 32 weeks PCA are capable of expressing pain through physiological measures and facial actions in a manner similar to more mature preterm and healthy term infants. While NIDCAP behaviors failed to reach statistical significance, this method may be helpful in providing information about the physiologic and behavioral cost of the heelstick event on preterm infants. The PIPP is a valid instrument for assessing pain in infants as young as 27-32 weeks PCA.

Keywords: pain; postconceptional age; premature newborn; heestick procedure; neonatal intensive care

From: Walden, M. (1997), *Changes over Six Weeks in Multivariate Responses of Premature Neonates to a Painful Stimulus.* Unpublished doctoral dissertation, The University of Texas at Austin, School of Nursing, Austin.

RESEARCH PLAN

A. Specific Aims

Each year in the United States, more than a quarter million infants are born with birth weights less than 2500 grams. Nearly 50,000 of these infants are born with very-low-birth weights (VLBW), less than 1500 grams (National Commission, 1990). These are the highest risk to survive infants. Als (1986) postulates that the persistence of subtle developmental impairments among preterm infants with essentially uncomplicated medical courses may be "the consequence of a mismatch of extrauterine environment and the capacity of the central nervous system of the fetal neonate which is adapted for an intrauterine existence" (p. 4). Characteristics of the Neonatal Intensive Care Unit (NICU), such as excessive and unpredictable **sound** levels, bright and/or continuous lighting, repeated and painful procedures are among the "mismatched of extrauterine" environmental stimuli Als refers to. These stimuli are potential challenges to the adaptive capacity of the preterm infant's central nervous system and are potentially detrimental to preterm development.

The purpose of this repeated measures study is to assess the relationship between three sets of variables: (a) **sound** and **light** levels in the NICU, (b) **arousal** level (sleep and wake patterns) of preterm infants, and (c) **physiologic** and **behavioral responses** of preterm infants to and following a **painful stimulus**—a heelstick for necessary blood sampling. Pain research in neonates has focused primarily on **behavioral** and **physiologic responses** to brief clinical procedures in healthy, full-term infants, and in older, physiologically stable preterm infants. No studies were located that have investigated the relationship of **sound** and **light** levels in the NICU and infant **arousal** level (sleep and wake patterns) to infant responses to pain.

Therefore, this study will examine the following research questions/hypotheses:

1. What is the relationship between **sound** (as measured by a sound meter), **light** (as measured by a light meter), **arousal** levels (as measured by Als State Score) in the 2 hours preceding a heelstick procedure to:

   A. Immediate **physiological pain response** of preterm neonates to a heelstick procedure (as measured by **heart rate** and **oxygen saturation**)?
   B. Immediate **behavioral pain responses** of preterm neonates to a heelstick procedure (as measured by the Premature Infant Pain Profile [**PIPP**])?

2. Is the relationship of **sound** (as measured by a sound meter), **light** (as measured by a light meter), **arousal** levels (as measured by Als State Score) in the 2 hours preceding a heelstick procedure moderated by **gestational age**?

3. Does variation in **sound** (as measured by a sound meter), **light** (as measured by a light meter), and **arousal** levels (as measured by Als State Score) in the 2 hours preceding a heelstick procedure predict:

   A. **Physiological disruption** from acute pain in preterm neonates (as measured by the **time for heart rate and oxygen saturation to return to baseline values).**
   B. **Behavioral disruption** from acute pain in preterm neonates following a heelstick procedure (as measured by **time for PIPP score to return to baseline value**).

4. Does **gestational age** interact with **sound** (as measured by a sound meter), **light** (as measured by a light meter), and **arousal** levels (as measured by Als State Score) in the 2 hours preceding a heelstick procedures in the prediction of:

   A. **Physiological disruption** from acute pain in preterm neonates (as measured by the **time for heart rate and oxygen saturation to return to baseline values**).

B. **Behavioral disruption** from acute pain in preterm neonates following a heelstick procedure (as measured by **time for PIPP score to return to baseline value**).

This research will systematically address the gaps in our knowledge about the relationships between **sound, light, arousal** levels (sleep and wake patterns), and preterm neonates' **physiological** and **behavioral responses** to painful clinical procedures. The long-term aims of this program of research are to investigate nursing interventions that promote an environment that produces optimal **arousal** patterns for high-risk neonates as indicated by minimizing preterm neonates' immediate response and prolonged **disruption** following painful procedures. The research may also permit improved understanding of how these factors may influence pain assessment in critically ill preterm neonates.

B. Background and Significance

Conceptual Framework

The framework for this study is a modification of the Middle-Range Theory of Unpleasant Symptoms. This model provides the overall conceptual framework for examining the relationship between **sound** and **light**, **arousal** levels (sleep and wake patterns), and **pain response** of preterm neonates in this study (Lenz, Pugh, Milligan, Gift, & Suppe, 1997). This model identifies three categories of variables as potentially influencing the intensity of the **pain response**: **physiologic**/developmental factors (**gestational age** at birth), psychologic factors (**arousal** levels [sleep and wake patterns]), and situational factors (**sound and light**). These categories are related and may interact to influence the symptom experience (**behavioral** and **physiologic response** to pain). Data will also be collected on other potential modifiers of the infant's **pain response** including postnatal age, acuity of illness, behavioral state just before the noxious stimuli, and previous pain experiences (total number of painful procedures and time since last painful procedure). Pain may result in short-term **physiologic** and/or **behavioral disruption** as well as long-term consequences including adverse neurologic and neurobehavioral outcomes and altered pain sensation. The long-term sequelae of pain are not the focus of this study. Rather, short-term **disruption** and disorganization will be measured as **physiological** manifestations (**time for heart rate and oxygen saturation to return to baseline**) and **behavioral** manifestations (**time for pain scores on PIPP to return to baseline**). Figure 1 presents a conceptual model of the relationship between the variables identified for study in this proposal.

Franck and Gregory (1993) state that "the goals of pain management in neonates are: (1) to minimize intensity, duration, and **physiologic** cost of the pain experience and (2) to maximize neonate's ability to cope with and recover from the painful experience" (p. 522). This suggests that NICU caregivers can assist neonates to cope with and recover from painful clinical procedures by promoting a healing environment that incorporates strategies to maximize sleep and waking patterns (arousal) and optimize **sound** and **light** levels in the NICU microenvironment. While clinical observation suggests that these factors influence infant responses to pain, no studies have examined the relationship of **sound** levels, **light** levels, and infant **arousal** (sleep and wake patterns) on infant's responses to painful clinical procedures. Our understanding of how these factors affect healing and recovery from painful stimuli may help to minimize long-term consequences of painful stimuli.

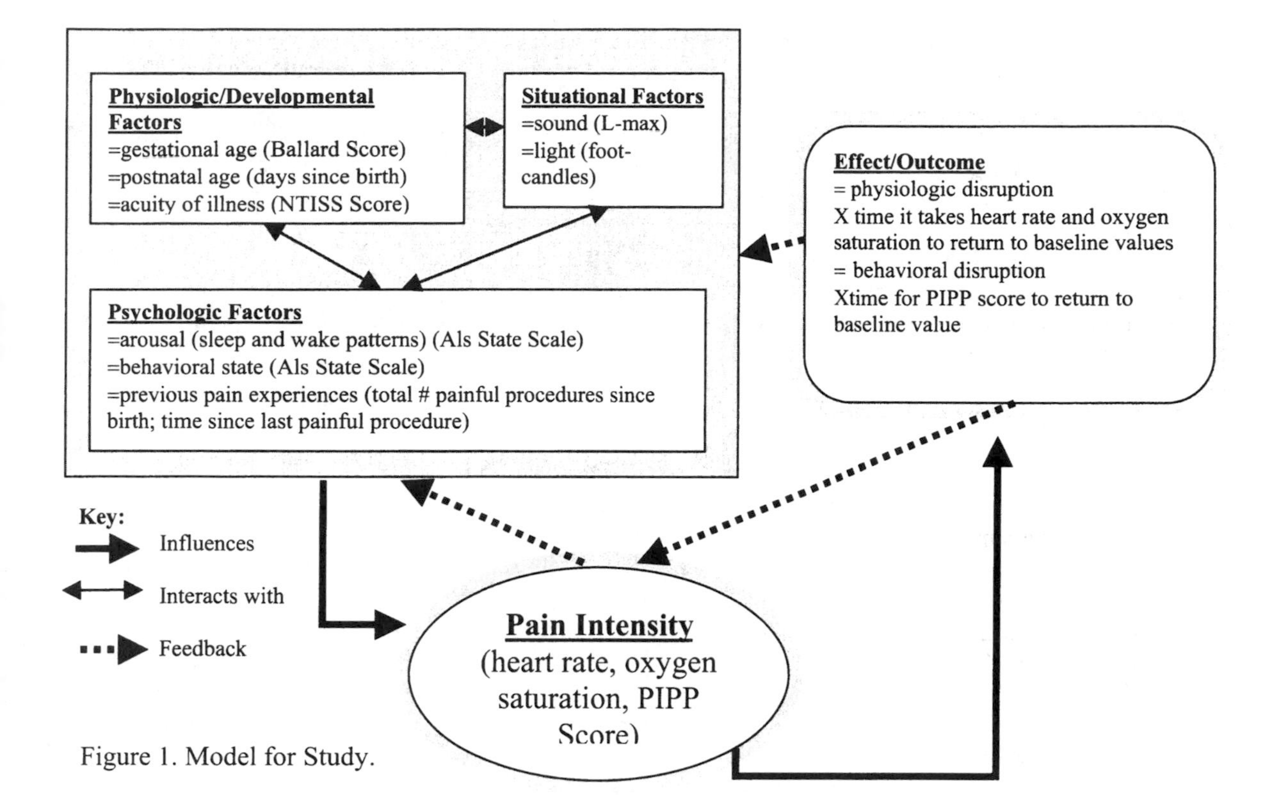

Figure 1. Model for Study.

Pain and the Pain Response

Painful procedures occur with relative frequency for preterm infants in the NICU. Barker and Rutter (1995) reported that preterm infants experienced an average of 61 painful procedures during their NICU stay, with increased frequency of procedures inversely related to **gestational age** and acuity of illness. One 23-week gestation, 560-gram infant had 488 procedures performed during her hospital stay. Studies have noted that neonates may be subjected to as many as three invasive procedures an hour (Pohlman & Beardslee, 1987).

Previously, preterm neonates were thought to be too immature to experience pain, but studies now confirm the preterm neonate's anatomic and functional capacity to respond to pain at birth (Anand, Phil, Grunau & Oberlander, 1997; Anand, Phil & Hickey, 1987; Fitzgerald & Anand, 1993). Acute **physiologic responses** to painful stimuli have been implicated as either causing or extending early intraventricular hemorrhage (IVH), or the development of ischemic changes leading to periventricular leukomalacia (PVL) in preterm neonates (Anand, 1998). New areas of concern suggest the cumulative effects of repeated painful medical procedures on the developing brain may be of greater biological and clinical importance than previously recognized (Anand, 1997; 1998; Anand, et al., 1997). Multiple lines of evidence suggest an increased sensitivity to pain in preterm neonates as compared to term infants (Anand, 1997; 1998; Fitzgerald, Shaw & MacIntosh, 1988). Evidence suggests that acute painful stimuli may lead to the development of prolonged periods of hyperalgesia and that non-noxious stimuli during periods of hyperalgesia may promote chronic pain in preterm neonates (Anand, 1997; 1998; Fitzgerald, et al., 1988). Preliminary data suggest that repetitive painful experiences in the NICU may be associated with some of the neurobehavioral and developmental sequelae in former preterm neonates, including altered pain thresholds and abnormal pain-related behaviors during early childhood (Grunau, Whitfield & Petrie, 1994; Gruanu, Whitfield, Petrie & Fryer, 1994).

Painful procedures in the NICU may be unavoidable; however, it is vital that caregivers investigate strategies to assist infants to cope with and recover from necessary but painful clinical procedures. Pain assessment is an essential prerequisite to optimal pain management. Pain research has produced several valid and reliable pain instruments, including the CRIES (Krechel & Bildner, 1995) and The Premature Infant Pain Profile (**PIPP**) (Stevens, B., Johnston, C., Petryshen, P., & Taddio, A., 1996). While the CRIES has been validated for use in infants greater than 32 weeks **gestational age**, the **PIPP** can be used in preterm infants below 28 weeks **gestational age**. The **PIPP** is preferred over the CRIES in this study as it controls for two significant contextual factors (**gestational age** and behavioral state) known to modify pain expression in preterm neonates (Craig, 1993; Grunau & Craig, 1987; Johnston, et al., 1999; Stevens & Johnston, 1994; Stevens, Johnston, & Horton, 1994). The **PIPP** will be used to measure acute **pain response** in this study.

Behavioral state has been shown to act as a moderator of **pain responses** in both full-term and preterm infants (Grunau & Craig; 1987; Johnston, et al., 1999; Stevens & Johnston, 1994; Stevens, et al., 1996). Infants in awake or alert states demonstrate a more robust reaction to painful stimuli than infants in sleep states. While clinical studies are lacking, a few laboratory studies have examined the impact of rapid eye movement (REM) sleep deprivation on pain thresholds using the rat model. Hicks, Coleman, Ferante, Sahatjian, and Hawkins (1979) and Hicks, Moore, Findley, Hirshfield, and Humphrey (1978) demonstrated that rats subjected to REM sleep deprivation showed significantly reduced pain thresholds which persisted for up to 96 hours following the termination of the REM deprivation. Another laboratory study used continuous polygraphic and behavioral recordings in freely moving cats to examine aspects of pain and sleep surrounding a persistent nociceptive stimulation (Carli, Montesano, Rapezzi, & Paluffi, 1987). These researchers demonstrated that the level of pain intensity following a formalin injection was inversely related to the duration of sleep disturbance. No clinical studies have examined the impact of **arousal** level (sleep and wake patterns) on the preterm neonate's ability to respond to and recover from painful procedures in the NICU.

Sound

Researchers have examined the immediate responses of infants to **sound** levels in the nursery. Long, Lucey, and Philips (1980) documented a repeated pattern of decreased transcutaneous oxygen tension, increased intracranial pressure, and increased heart and respiratory rates in two infants in response to sudden loud noise in the nursery. Gorski, et al. (1983) described mottling, apnea, and bradycardia in preterm infants exposed to sharp occurrences of **sound** such as telephone ringing, monitor alarms, and conversation during medical rounds. Both studies provide support for the notion that nursery **sound** levels are a disorganizing influence on the neurologically immature low-birth-weight infant and raise speculation regarding the energy cost to the infant that these episodes represent. Noise intensity decreased by 10 decibels resulted in longer sleep time in healthy preterm neonates (Mann, Haddon, Stokes, Goodley & Rulter, 1986). When studying the effects of noise on the sleep patterns of term infants, Gadeke, Doing, Keller, and Vogel (1969) reported that **sound** levels of greater than 70 decibels disrupted infant sleep and **sound** levels of 55 decibels aroused an infant from light sleep. Although this study has not been replicated with LBW infants, the reported **sound** levels are similar to those present in the NICU, suggesting that **sound** may interfere with the development of sleep and rest patterns in these infants. Almost no research has been done systematically to document the relationship between **sound** levels and **pain responses** in preterm infants. Using a subjective scale to rate **sound** levels from one to nine, Walden (1997) failed to demonstrate a significant association between **sound** and **pain responses** in hospitalized preterm infants. Failure to achieve significance may have been due, in part, to the subjective nature of the measurement scale. Further research is needed using a sound meter to measure systematically the relationship between **sound** levels (Lmax) and the response pattern of preterm infants to painful clinical procedures. Again, this research may lead to improved assessment techniques for pain in critically ill preterm neonates as well as stimulate intervention research to better control **sound** levels in the NICU surrounding painful procedures.

Light

The NICU provides infants with an extremely bright environment with little diurnal variation (Lotas & Walden, 1996). Shiroiwa, Kamiya, and Uchiboi (1986) reported a significant association between lighting levels and patterns of alertness and respiratory stability in neonates. Studies exploring the effects of light/dark cycles on preterm infant **physiologic** and **behavioral** functioning have reported decreased **heart rate**, decreased respiratory rate, and improved sleep patterns and weight gain (Blackburn & Patterson, 1991; Mann, et al., 1986). While continuous lighting patterns have been hypothesized to contribute to sleep disruption during the NICU stay (Holditch-Davis, 1998), little research exists that systematically documents the effects of ambient **light** levels on **pain responses** in preterm infants. Walden (1997) failed to demonstrate a significant association between ratings of **light** levels in the NICU on subjective scale and **physiologic** and **behavioral responses** of preterm infants to a heelstick procedure. Here again, failure to achieve significance may have been due, in part, to the subjective nature of the measurement scale. Further research is needed, using a more objective measure furnished by light meter recordings (foot-candles) to explore the effects of NICU **light** on **pain responses** of hospitalized preterm neonates. Again, this research may lead to improved assessment techniques for pain in critically ill preterm neonates as well as stimulate intervention research to reduce **light** levels and patterns in the NICU surrounding painful clinical procedures.

Arousal Level (Sleep and **Wake Patterns)**

Adequate rest is a prerequisite for optimal recovery from acute and chronic conditions. Preterm infants require more sleep than adults and, in general, spend as much as 60–70% of the day in sleep (Holditch-Davis, 1998). In the normal intrauterine environment, this amount of undisturbed time is routine; in the NICU, it is not. Nursing and medical interventions in the NICU of five times per hour have been reported (Duxbury, Henly, Broz, Armstrong, & Wachdorf, 1984). A recent study states that preterm infants are handled a mean of 113 times per 24 hours, with undisturbed rest periods of between 2 and 59 minutes (Appleton, 1997). Frequent handling has been associated with hypoxemia, tachycardia, bradycardia, tachypnea, apnea, and increased intracranial pressures in critically ill neonates (Cooper-Evans, 1991; Gorski, et al., 1983; Long, Lucey & Philips, 1980; Murdoch & Darlow, 1984; Norris, Campbell & Brenkert, 1982; Peters, 1992). Several researchers suggest that hypoxic episodes in response to handling may actually be the result of changes in sleeping and waking states (Gottfried, 1985; Holditch-Davis, 1998; Speidel, 1978). Routine caregiving may also interfere with development of normal sleep patterns, which are important for neurologic organization and growth (Appleton, 1997; Jorgensen, 1993; Wolke, 1987). Seventy-eight percent of changes in sleep-wake states in preterm neonates are associated with either nursing interventions or NICU noise (Zahr & Balian, 1995). Holditch-Davis (1990, 1998) reported that frequent nursing interventions reduce the amount of quiet sleep that preterm infants experience. In contrast, quiet periods in the NICU with reduced noise and light levels have been demonstrated to reduce stress responses in sick newborns (Slevin, Farrington, Duffy, Daly, and Murphy, 2000). No research that we could find has investigated the relationship of extended infant **arousal** levels (sleep and wake patterns) in the NICU and pain assessment in critically ill preterm neonates. In addition to improved assessment opportunities, this research may lead to the development of nursing interventions to promote optimal **arousal** (sleep and wake patterns) in the NICU. This will help preterm neonates recover from postoperative, procedural, and/or disease-related pain experiences.

Physiologic Responses

Studies of fullterm as well as preterm infants provide evidence that they exhibit **physiological responses** to a heelstick procedure. Limited research suggests that preterm infants respond to noxious stimuli in patterns similar to that of fullterm neonates, including increases in **heart rate** (Bozzette, 1993; Craig, et al., 1993; McIntosh, et al., 1994; Stevens & Johnston, 1994; Stevens, et al., 1993; Walden, 1997) and decreases in **oxygen saturation** (Craig, et al., 1993; Stevens & Johnston, 1994; Stevens, et al., 1993; Walden, 1997).

Fullterm infants demonstrate slight **physiologic** distress persisting into a relatively brief recovery period following a heelstick procedure. Owens and Todt (1984) demonstrated an increased mean **heart rate** for 3.5 minutes following the heelstick procedure in fullterm newborns. Beaver (1987) demonstrated a trend for increased **heart rates** for from 1 to 1.5 minutes post-heelstick in a small sample of preterm infants. Sustained elevations in **heart rate** and reduced transcutaneous oxygen levels attest to the persistent effect of the heelstick procedures on the **physiologic** stability of preterm infants (Craig, et al., 1993; Stevens, et al., 1993). Walden (1997) demonstrated that preterm neonates at 27 weeks postconceptional age had persistent increases in mean **heart rate** for up to 4 minutes following the heelstick itself (actual stick), while significantly elevated mean maximum **heart rates** persisted for up to 8 minutes following the heelstick procedure. Further research with longer observation of recovery intervals is needed in order to investigate more thoroughly the lasting impact of acute procedure-induced pain on the **physiologic** parameters of **heart rate** and **oxygen saturation** in preterm neonates. This study will monitor **physiologic responses** for 1 hour post-heelstick procedure to note **physiologic disruption** from acute pain in preterm neonates (as measured by **time for heart rate and oxygen saturation to return to baseline values**).

Behavioral Response

While behavioral state has been shown to act as a moderator of **behavioral pain responses** in both full-term and preterm infants (Grunau & Craig, 1987; Stevens & Johnston, 1994; Stevens, Johnston, Petryshen, & Taddio, 1996), the research has primarily examined the immediate effects of the infant's sleep-wake state on **physiologic** and **behavioral responses** to pain. A limited number of human studies have reported that noxious procedures in neonates result in **behavioral responses** of increased sleep disruption times, particularly crying time, during and immediately following the painful event (Corff, Seideman, Venkataraman, Lutes, & Yates, 1995; Field & Goldson, 1984; Holditch-Davis & Calhoun, 1989; Van Cleve, et al., 1995). We could find no studies examining the influence of disturbed sleep and wake patterns several hours preceding a clinical procedure on the preterm neonate's ability to respond to and recover from clinically needed, painful procedures experienced in the NICU.

Research examining facial and body activity has demonstrated that the magnitude of infant's **behavioral response** to pain is less vigorous and robust with decreasing post-conceptional age (Craig, et al., 1993; Johnston, et al., 1995; Johnston, et al., 1999). These observations, however, are contrary to data which suggest that more immature preterm infants have a lower threshold and are hypersensitive to painful stimuli compared to older preterm neonates (Andrews & Fitzgerald, 1994; Fitzgerald, et al., 1989). Craig, et al. (1993) suggest that the less vigorous **behavioral responses** demonstrated by younger preterm infants "should be interpreted in the context of the energy resources available to respond and the relative immaturity of the musculoskeletal system" (p. 296). Stratification of infants into two groups by **gestational age** (25-27 weeks **gestational age** at birth and 34-36 weeks **gestational age** at birth) will permit systematic investigation for the presence of an interaction effect of **gestational age** on the relationships between environmental variables (**sound** and **light**) and **pain response** and **recovery**.

Furthermore, emerging evidence suggest that NICU experience may produce altered **behavioral responses** to noxious stimuli as the total number of invasive procedures that a preterm infant encounters increases with advancing postnatal age (Johnston & Stevens, 1996). More recently, Johnston, et al. (1999) found that postnatal age at time of study, **gestational age** at birth, time since last painful procedure, and behavioral state predict response to a heel stick procedure in preterm neonates. Therefore, this study will systematically collect data on behavioral state just prior to the heelstick procedure. In addition, data will also be collected on the total number of painful procedures and time since last painful procedure. This information will help to describe better the previous pain experiences of the study sample. Data will also be collected within the first postnatal week in order to control for the influence of postnatal age on **pain responses** of preterm neonates.

Summary

Nurses play an important role in effectively implementing nonpharmacologic approaches to pain management. Research supports the use of hand swaddling (often referred to as "facilitated tucking", Corff, et al., 1995), nonnutritive sucking (Marchette, Main, & Redick, 1991; Campos, 1989; Shiao, Chang, Lannon, & Yarandi, 1997; Field and Goldson, 1984; Miller and Anderson; 1993; Stevens, et al., 1999), and sucrose pacifiers (Stevens, Taddio, Ohlsson, & Einarson, 1997; Johnston, Stremler, Stevens, & Horton, 1997; Stevens & Ohlsson, 1998) as nonpharmacologic therapies in newborns. However, virtually no research has been done to systematically document the effects of **sound, light**, and **arousal** levels on **pain responses** in preterm infants. Our understanding of how **sound, light**, and **arousal** levels influence the infant's ability to respond to and recover from painful procedures will provide improved assessment of pain in critically ill preterm neonates. Moreover, this improved understanding will permit caregivers to develop interventions to modify the NICU microenvironment a manner that minimizes infant acute **physiologic** and **behavioral responses** to pain and thereby help to decrease long-term neurobehavioral sequelae of chronic, repetitive pain experiences. Data from this study will provide the necessary information and objective clinical data methods to develop and apply for a competitive R01 grant to design and assess an intervention study.

C. Preliminary Studies

Dr. Marlene Walden, principal investigator (PI) is an Assistant Professor at the University of Texas Medical Branch (UTMB) in Galveston and a recent graduate of The University of Texas at Austin (UTA), School of Nursing. Dr. Walden's doctoral dissertation, *Changes over six weeks in multivariate responses of premature neonates to a painful stimulus"* won the UTA School of Nursing Outstanding Doctoral Dissertation Award. This research also received funding support from the Foundation for Neonatal Research and Education and was awarded the Department of Nursing Research Award from Texas Children's Hospital. A database manuscript has been submitted and is included as **Appendix A.**

Walden (1997) studied the **physiologic** and **behavioral responses** of preterm infants to a routinely administered **painful stimulus** (heelstick for necessary blood sampling) at weekly intervals between ages 27-32 weeks postconceptional age The Neonatal Individualized Developmental Care Assessment Program (NIDCAP) method was used with a nonprobability convenience sample of 11 preterm infants born at 24-26 weeks postconceptional age who were admitted to one of two NICUs. Univariate **physiologic** indicators of pain included **heart rate**, **oxygen saturation**, and respiratory rate. These measures were collected in a time-sampling fashion in two-minute intervals. Results demonstrated that **heart rate** increased while **oxygen saturation** and respiratory rate decreased during the most invasive phase (heelstick). While the trends of these findings were in the direction demonstrated in research with other preterm populations, they failed to achieve significance across all postconceptional ages. In addition, correlations between **physiologic** indicators, **PIPP** scores, and NICU **sound** and **light** levels (as measured by subjective scales) failed to demonstrate significant associations. Further investigation of these findings is needed using a larger sample size to provide (a) the necessary power for analyses in a rigorous study, and (b) more objective measurement of **sound** and **light** levels. Such data and subsequent analyses and results are needed to examine contextual factors that may modify pain response and recovery in critically ill preterm neonates as well as to design intervention studies that may help neonates cope with painful clinical procedures. Specifically, optimizing **sound**, **light**, and **arousal** levels in the NICU may be found as fruitful means to alter the neonate's response to and recovery from painful procedures. Data and experiences from the PI's previous study provide preparation to conduct pain research in critically ill preterm neonates and to examine the variables of interest in this proposed research study.

Dr. Walden's research experience relates directly to the proposed project in terms of content and clinical experience and familiarity with the setting and study population. Her expertise in neonatal pain has been recognized by numerous invitations to speak on the topic at national neonatal conferences and most recently as the invited author to write the pain assessment and management guidelines for The National Association of Neonatal Nurses. She has also acquired expertise in data collection methods through a Faculty Scientist Award for Pain in Neonates from

Nell Hodgson Woodruff School of Nursing, Emory University, where she consulted under Dr. Jane Evans and Dr. Terese Verklan, both currently funded by NIH. Dr. Walden gained experience in that setting for the use of data acquisition methods in neonatal research. In addition, Dr. Walden is currently serving as a data collector using **physiologic** data acquisition methods for Dr. Terese Verklan's currently funded R01 study, "Heart Rate During Transition to Extrauterine Life".

The research team for this study was carefully selected to provide the expertise necessary to conduct a rigorous scientific study. The research team members' expertise is briefly summarized below.

Joan Smith, RN, MSN, CNS (Co-Investigator) is currently a Clinical Nurse Specialist for the Newborn Center at Texas Children's Hospital. She has conducted several quality improvement projects to analyze **sound** and **light** levels in the Newborn Center, including the design, data collection, analysis, and dissemination of findings to administration and other medical and nursing colleagues. The quality improvement projects she has conducted have used the same light meter and a similar sound meter that will be used to collect data in this study. The data from her quality improvement projects will be used to describe the environment of the Newborn Center under study setting. Ms. Smith also has an excellent repertoire with families and the health care team and has familiarity and experience in site coordination for medical studies as well as collecting informed consents from parents.

Dr. Jean Smithers (Consultant) is an Associate Professor at the University of Texas-Health Science Center at Houston, School of Nursing. Dr. Smithers is a Clinical Nurse Specialist in high-risk neonatal care. Her dissertation was conducted at the University of Pennsylvania, under the direction of Dr. Barbara Medoff-Cooper, PhD, FAAN. This research investigated if a pattern of neurophysiologic maturation exists in association with increasing **gestational age**. **Heart rate** variability was examined in infants at 28-, 32-, and 40-weeks postconceptional age while controlling for behavioral state. The results demonstrated a discernable pattern of neurophysiologic growth with increasing **gestational age**. Dr. Smithers has completed two additional studies with similar aims that have built on the findings from her doctoral dissertation. Her current R01 study examines the differences/similarities in **heart rate** variability in the same individual as s/he experiences labor, delivery (fetus→neonate), immediately at birth, and the first ten hours of extrauterine life.

Dr. Alan Brown is a Professor at the University of Texas Medical Branch at Galveston, School of Nursing and Department of Preventive Medicine and Community Health. Dr. Brown is a senior biostatistian for the Office of Biostatistics and the Office for Nursing Research and Scholarship at UTMB. His current research involves aspects of social cognitive theory. In addition, Dr. Brown has extensive experience in serving on research teams and assisting faculty in developing research designs and statistical plans for data management, analysis, and interpretation.

Timothy Jones, is an Associate Professor in Health Related Studies and currently serves as the Associate Director of the Biomedical Engineering and Electronics Department at UTMB. Mr. Jones is directly responsible for the day-to-day operations involving the support of patient care and laboratory equipment at UTMB, a 900-bed teaching hospital. He also provides design and fabrication services to meet various research needs at UTMB. Mr. Jones will be responsible for assisting in the purchase, set-up, and pilot testing of the data acquisition system required to measure the **physiological** and environmental variables within this study. He will also provide consultation regarding any trouble-shooting of equipment malfunctions that may occur during the data collection period.

A research assistant will be hired to assist primarily in data collection. A currently enrolled Registered Nurse with at least two years of NICU experience will be targeted from the RN to BSN or master's student population. An experienced neonatal nurse is required due to the high-risk patient population and special knowledge and skills to handle these acutely ill neonates. The Faculty-student relationship will be used to mentor the student in both research and clinical skills and will serve as a mechanism to provide encouragement and support for the student to pursue an advanced nursing degree. In addition, as an active member of the research team, the student will gain valuable experience in conducting research studies in the clinical setting. University and

Hospital relations between faculty, administrators, and bedside clinicians will be emphasized for the purpose of promoting clinical scholarship and research utilization projects at the bedside.

D. Research Design and Methods

Design

A repeated measures study will be employed, using a naturalistic design, to assess the relationship between **sound**, **light** and **arousal** levels in the 2 hours before a noxious clinical procedure, and **physiologic** and **behavioral responses** to a routinely administered, **painful stimulus** (heelstick for blood sampling). Infants in this study will be stratified into two **gestational age** at birth groups: 25-27 weeks and 34-36 weeks. Rapid development and maturation of the nervous system occurs during the third trimester of pregnancy and is expected to be associated with systematic and substantial changes in the **physiologic** and **behavioral responses** of preterm neonates to painful clinical procedures. Stratification into two groups will determine if a moderating interaction is present when the relationship between two variables (e.g., **sound** and **pain response** or **recovery**) is different at levels of a third variable (e.g., **gestational age**).

We will observe the **physiological** and **behavioral responses** of neonates during a heelstick period during the first week of postnatal age. Heelstick observation periods will consist of the following three phases: (a) pre-heelstick observation (2 hours before the heelstick), (b) heelstick procedure (variable duration, from lance to placement of Band-Aid), and (c) post-heelstick recovery observation (1 hour). Thus, there will be systematic data collection from three observation intervals across two age-stratified groups of infants (3 X 2 design).

Setting and Sample

The setting for this study will be the Newborn Center at Texas Children's Hospital (TCH), a large tertiary care nursery located in the Texas Medical Center in Houston, Texas. TCH is approximately 65 miles from UTMB School of Nursing. This site was chosen due to the large number of potentially eligible infants admitted each year. Due to the distance between UTMB and TCH, a site coordinator was selected to assist with subject enrollment and site management. PI travel to the site is not anticipated as a problem as the PI's residence is very close to TCH. Student research assistant travel similarly is not anticipated to be problematic as a large number of the RN to BSN and master's students in the UTMB program live in the Houston area.

Ms. Carrier has conducted several quality improvement projects on **sound** and **light** levels in the Newborn Center at TCH. The **sound** levels in the Newborn Center average 64.9 (Lmax). The minimum **sound** level is on average 63.3 (Lmax) with a minimum average equivalent level of 58.8 Leq. The average maximum level is 89.8 (Lmax), with occasional peaks to as high as 108.5 (Lmax).

Measurements of **light** levels have also been obtained for the Newborn Center at TCH. With overhead lighting, **light** levels range from 70.5 –79.8 foot-candles (ftc). With lights on, **light** levels in an incubator with a thin blanket average 60.3 ftc and with a thick cover 19.3 ftc. In an incubator in dim lighting with no cover, the **light** levels average 4.9 ftc. When lights are turned off, **light** levels in an incubator with a thin blanket average 0.9 ftc and with thick covering 0.3 ftc.

This study uses a repeated measures, naturalistic design. No attempt will be made to manipulate the independent variables of **sound** and **light** in this study. The purpose of this study is to explore the relationships of **sound** and **light** levels in the NICU in the 2 hours preceding a heelstick procedure and **infant responses to pain**.

Participation of Children

All subjects will be children, specifically premature neonates, as the research questions are particularly pertinent to this age group. Enrollment of neonates born at **gestational age** greater than 36 weeks would not provide the data necessary to answer the specific age related questions raised. The intensive care nursery at TCH admits approximately 185 infants per year in the respective age groups of this study. The bed capacity in the Newborn Care Center is 120 beds. This setting is expected to produce sufficient numbers for the sample based on inclusion and exclusion criteria.

Total time for data collection is not expected to exceed 15 months. The PI and co-investigator have over 39 combined years experience in working with the study population of high-risk premature infants. Because of the knowledge and expertise required to handle complex acutely ill infants, the student research assistant to be recruited will also be required to have at least two years of neonatal care experience.

Gender and Minority Inclusion

There will be no exclusion criteria related to gender, therefore an enrollment of approximately 35% females and 65% males is expected. These percentages represent the actual gender representation in the Newborn Center population at TCH in 1999. The following Table provides distribution by gender and racial/ethnic categories:

	Male	Female	Black, not of Hispanic Origin	Hispanic	White, not of Hispanic Origin	Other or Unknown	Total
25-27 weeks	45	21	20	16	29	1	66
34-36 weeks	75	44	20	38	58	3	119
Total	120	65	40	54	87	4	185

All infants admitted to the Newborn Care Center at TCH will be considered eligible for inclusion into the study if the following criteria are met: (a) infants between 25-27 weeks or 34-36 weeks **gestational age** at birth and appropriate for **gestational age** as determined by the New Ballard Score (Ballard, Khoury, Wedig, Wang, Eilers-Walsman & Lipp, 1991); (b) scheduled to receive a routine heelstick procedure within the first postnatal week.

Exclusion criteria include: (a) chromosomal or genetic anomalies; (b) significant central nervous system abnormality including seizures or a Grade III/IV intraventricular hemorrhage; (c) infants born to mothers with a known history of substance abuse; (d) infants who receive paralytic, analgesic, or sedating medications within 24 hours before the heelstick procedure.

A convenience sample of consecutively admitted infants (stratified into two equal **gestational age** groups: 25-27 weeks and 34-36 weeks) who meet the subject criteria will be recruited for enrollment from the accessible population. Enrollment will continue until 102 infants' parents consent to participation and the research protocol is completed on those infants. Sample size for the study was determined using PASS 2000 (Hintze, 2000) and based on the most conservative estimate of sample size to answer the research questions in this study (multiple regression power analyses = 51/group). Because no data exist to estimate effect size outcomes in this case, a medium effect size was selected (R-Squared = 0.13) for main effects and a small to medium effect size (R-Squared = 0.09) for interaction terms, i.e. **gestational age** group by **sound**, **light**, and **arousal** levels). The data gathered in this project would allow a more informed selection of an effect size in developing future study designs, for example, an intervention study to follow-up on findings from this research. The following assumptions were used to perform the power analysis: (a) there will be three predictor variables (**sound** [mean Lmax value for preheelstick interval], **light** [mean foot-candles value for preheelstick interval], **arousal** [mean of Als states scored every two minutes during preheelstick interval]); (b) statistical power is set at .80; (c) level of significance in this study is set at $p \leq .05$. Under these assumptions, sample size was calculated at 51. To allow for possible differences between subgroups in the multiple regression analyses, 51 subjects will be enrolled for each subgroup (25-27 weeks and 34-36 weeks **gestational age**). Subject recruitment and enrollment procedures will continue until 51 infants are recruited in each **gestational age** group for a total sample size of 102.

Study Instruments

Three standardized instruments will be used to measure **physiologic** and **behavioral responses** to pain: the infant's bedside SpaceLabs Cardiorespiratory Monitor, Nellcor Pulse Oximeter, and the **PIPP**. **Sound** and **light** levels will be collected using a Quest Technologies Sound Meter and Extech Light Meter, respectively. In addition, the neonate's **arousal** level will be measured with Al's State Scoring System. Data from all instruments will be recorded simultaneously by an on-site study computer.

The New Ballard Score will be used to determine eligibility for inclusion in the study based on **gestational age** at birth. Severity of illness will be measured using the Neonatal Therapeutic Intervention Scoring System. Finally, demographic data will be collected using the Naturalistic Observation of Newborn Behavior Instrument.

Physiological Responses (Heart Rate, Oxygen Saturation): The infant's SpaceLabs cardiorespiratory monitor will measure the infant's **heart rate**. Three neonatal body surface electrodes will be attached to the skin using two mid-axillary chest positions and one left lateral abdominal position. Quality ECG recording will be assured before data collection. The SpaceLabs monitor has an accuracy of $\pm$ 2 beats per minute averaged over 3 seconds.

Oxygen saturation will be recorded continuously using a Nellcor Pulse Oximeter module programmed within the SpaceLabs cardiorespiratory monitor. Reliability of the pulse oximeter reading will be verified by noting the congruence between the pulse oximeter digital reading for **heart rate** and that of the reading on the infant's cardiac monitor. In infants, the correlation between transcutaneous estimates and measured arterial saturations approaches an *r*-value of 0.91 using the Nellcor pulse oximeter (Fanconi, 1988).

Analog signals from **physiologic** parameters will be captured, digitized, synchronized, and stored using a desktop computer and National Instruments Data Acquisition System. All caregiving events as well as significant environmental happenings occurring during data collection for infants will be noted corresponding to an electronic event marker notation on the desktop computer.

Premature Infant Pain Profile (PIPP): Since pain is a multidimensional phenomenon, a multi-dimensional approach should be employed to study pain (U.S. Department of Health and Human Services, 1992). The **PIPP**, developed by Stevens and colleagues (1996) is a composite measure of pain in preterm infants < 28 weeks through 40 weeks **gestational age (see Appendix B)**. The **PIPP** scores on a four-point scale the variables of **heart rate**, **oxygen saturation**, brow bulge, eye squeeze, nasolabial furrow, **gestational age** and behavioral state. The sum of scores for each of the scales equals a total pain score. Internal consistency of the **PIPP** was estimated with the standardized item alpha of 0.71. Construct validity of the measure was supported using a contrasting groups approach in three samples of preterm and term infants. Ballantyne, Stevens, McAllister, Dionne, and Jack (1999) showed interrater reliability between two independent raters of 0.93 - 0.96 and intrarater reliability between bedside ratings and videotape ratings of 0.94 - 0.98. For the purposes of this study, the **PIPP** will be scored during the first 30 seconds of each 2-minute interval during data collection.

Sound Levels: Continuous **sound** levels will be measured using Quest Technologies Integrating/Datalogging Sound Level Meter (Model 2900). The accuracy of this Type 2 meter is estimated at +/- 2%. The microphone will be suspended from the infant's bed (radiant warmer, incubator, or crib) and placed in direct proximity to the infant's ears. The sound level meter will be calibrated before each data collection period and set to record maximum (L-max) levels.

Light Levels: Continuous ambient **light** levels will be measured in foot-candles using Extech Heavy Duty Light Meter (Model # 407026). The recording meter will be placed in direct proximity to the infant's bed (radiant warmer, incubator, or crib), adjacent to the infant's head, and at the level of the infant's eyes. The meter will be calibrated before each data collection period. Selecting the lighting type enhances reliability of the readings: fluorescent, sodium, tungsten/daylight, or mercury. The light selection procedure will be used for data collection. The Extech Heavy Duty Light Meter has been determined to be accurate within a $\pm$ 5% error range.

Als State Scoring System: Als State Scoring System (Als, et al., 1986) is a 13-state system used in the Neonatal Individualized Developmental Assessment Program (NIDCAP) specifically designed to measure sleeping and waking states of preterm infants. These sleep and wake patterns represent the **arousal** level variable. The scoring system is widely used in neonatal research (Als, et al., 1986; Corff, et al., 1995; Walden, 1997) and has been shown to correlate with electro**physiologic** measures of brain activity (Holditch-Davis, 1998). The 13 sleep-wake state categories can be reduced into six **arousal** categories as follows: state 1 = deep sleep; state 2 = light sleep; state 3 = drowsiness; state 4 = awake, alert; state 5 = aroused, fussy; and state 6 = crying.

During the time between the 2 hours preceding the heelstick to application of the Band-Aid following the heelstick procedure, sleep-wake states will be scored every 2 minutes. Scores involve observing a 30-second interval (i.e. the last 30 seconds of every 2-minute interval) and scoring the highest behavioral state that was attained during that interval **(see Appendix C).** A synchronized nonaudible timer (Radio Shack's Big Digit Timer) will be used to indicate the two-minute intervals for the recording of sleep/wake data. The state will be immediately placed into the database by using the corresponding numbered key on the computer. For data analysis, Als sleep-wake state categories will be averaged over the 2-hour preheelstick observation period to create an **arousal** score between 1 and 6.

New Ballard Score (NBS) (Newborn Maturity Rating and Classification Assessment): The NBS will determine eligibility for enrollment in the study based on **gestational age** at birth **(see Appendix D)**. The NBS is a 13-category scale designed to assess neuromuscular and physical maturity of neonates at 0 to 96 hours of life (Ballard, et al., 1991). The maturity rating is evaluated on a 1 to 5 scale, with the total range of scores from -10 to 50 indicating a **gestational age** of 20 to 44 weeks, respectively. In the Ballard study, validity of the NBS was supported by correlations between **gestational age** by last menstrual period (confirmed by agreement within two weeks with **gestational age** by prenatal ultrasonography) and NBS scores. For the 530 infants studied, interrater reliability was documented by correlation between raters who rated the same infants ($r = 0.95$).

Neonatal Therapeutic Intervention Scoring System (NTISS): The NTISS (Gray, Richardson, McCormick, Workman-Daniels & Goldmann, 1992) will be used to determine the acuity of illness in preterm infants participating in the study **(see Appendix E).** The therapeutic intensity and complexity for various intensive care therapies is rated per medical record review. Eight clinical subscores are included on the NTISS and consist of respiratory, cardiovascular, drug therapy, monitoring, metabolic/nutrition, transfusion, procedural, and vascular access. The daily NTISS score is computed as the sum of therapy points received by a patient in a 24-hour period. Scores range from 0 to 47, and the higher the score, the greater the **physiologic** instability and severity of illness. Because study infants may not have certain laboratory work ordered on days that data are collected, the NTISS is more useful in determining severity of illness than other scales that depend on extensive blood/lab value calculations to determine severity of illness. In development of the NTISS instrument, internal consistency using Cronbach's alpha was estimated at 0.84. Convergent validity was supported by correlations between NTISS scores and mortality risk estimates for neonates by neonatal attending physicians ($r = 0.70, p < 0.0001$), and a measure of nursing acuity ($r = 0.69, p < 0.0001$).

Naturalistic Observation of Newborn Behavior Instrument (NONB): The Naturalistic Observation of Newborn Behavior Instrument (Als, 1984) will be used to collect demographic data on all participants in the study **(See Appendix F)**. Data obtained from the NONB include maternal history, infant history including complications, current status including respiratory function, medications, mode of feeding, current medical problems, and current observation circumstances including type of bed, facilitation devices in use, and caregiver activity. This is a commonly used instrument in neonatal research (Als, et al., 1986; Walden, 1997). Data from the NONB will be used to describe the sample. Additional demographic information to be obtained will include the number and type of painful procedures performed from birth until the heelstick observation period and the time since the last painful event. For this study, data on painful procedures will be collected using the infant's medical record and will include heelstick, intravenous line insertion, venipuncture, lumbar puncture, percutaneous central line insertion, percutaneous arterial puncture, chest tube insertion/removal, central line placement/removal, endotracheal intubation, or a surgical procedure. Time since last painful event will also be collected from the infant's medical record and will involve the timing between any of the above procedures and the lance during heelstick data collection period.

Data Collection Procedure

The Site Coordinator will make daily rounds in the Newborn Care Center at TCH to identify eligible subjects. After eligibility criteria have been confirmed, the Principal Investigator or Site Coordinator will contact the parent(s) for informed consent. Eligible infants will be assigned nonrandomly to one of two groups based on **gestational age** at birth: a) Group 1 will consist of 51 preterm infants 25-27 weeks **gestational age**; b) Group 2 will consist of 51 preterm neonates 34-36 weeks **gestational age** at birth. This grouping is for data analysis purposes only. There are no differences between the groups in the procedures used for data collection.

Data collection will occur within the first postnatal week and will begin two hours before a scheduled heelstick procedure. Heelsticks are typically performed on a routine schedule when a neonate has a standing order for such procedures, as is the case in the eligible neonates, thus facilitating data collection. All measurements will be collected during the routine laboratory collection times. Caregiving activities will not be systematically altered in order to record the infant's routine NICU experiences surrounding the heelstick procedure. The PI has used this approach in previous research and it was found feasible within the NICU environment.

A standardized nonpharmacologic comfort measure will be provided throughout the data collection period. This comfort measure will be initiated at the start of data collection and involves maintaining the infant in the side lying position using a Bendy Bumper (Children's Medical Ventures). The Bendy Bumper provides for motoric containment of the infant's arms and legs in a flexed, midline position. This type of nonpharmacologic comfort measure is now in use with preterm infants in many neonatal units across the country. It is currently the standard of care in the data collection site (TCH). While other nonpharmacologic measures will not be systematically instituted, the research assistant will record, using the on-site computer database, any other nonpharmacologic pain measure that is provided by the infant's caregiver.

During each heelstick observation period, the data signal for **physiologic** variables (**heart rate** and **oxygen saturation**) will be captured using the bedside computer and National Instruments Data Acquisition System, LabView. The data acquisition cable from the analogue-digital board will be connected to the R232 port at the back of the infant's bedside SpaceLabs cardiorespiratory monitor. The analogue-digital board will be used for the purpose of synchronization, digitization and storage of data on the computer's zip drive. The infant's ECG wires and pulse oximeter probe will not be relocated unless an adequate signal cannot be obtained for data acquisition. At the start of data collection, the Extech Heavy Duty Light Meter (Model # 407026) will be calibrated and placed in direct proximity to the infant's bed (radiant warmer, incubator, or crib), adjacent to the infant's head, and at the level of the infant's eyes. The Quest Technologies Data Logging Sound Meter (Model 2900) microphone will be calibrated and suspended from the infant's bed (radiant warmer, incubator, or crib) and placed in direct proximity to the infant's ears. The **sound** and **light** meters will be connected to an on-site study computer via the analogue-digital board for synchronization, digitization, and storage of data. Infant **arousal** levels will be recorded during the last thirty seconds of every two minutes using the Als State Scoring System (1986). A timer (Radio Shack's Big Digit Timer) which is synchronized to correspond with continuous data collection instrumentation will be used to note the start of every two-minute interval. A **PIPP** score will be obtained during the first 30 seconds of each 2-minute interval throughout the data collection procedure.

Whenever possible, the selection of the heel will be accomplished by randomization by the research assistant by flipping a coin. The lab technician will perform the heelstick procedure according to a standard protocol. To standardize the procedure, the infant's heel will be randomly selected prior to data collection. Following the preheelstick observation period, the laboratory technician or research assistant will place the heel warmer on the randomized heel for two minutes. The laboratory technician will then start the heel lance procedure at the beginning of a two-minute interval by picking up the infant's foot and swabbing the heel with alcohol. The heel will be lanced using a spring-loaded incision device (Microtainer Brand Safety Flow Lancet, Becton Dickinson and Company, Rutherford, NJ) which makes a uniform incision 2.5 mm in length and 1.0 mm in depth on the lateral area of the heel. Subsequently, the technician will squeeze the heel, only repeating the lance procedure as necessary to draw sufficient blood. This process will continue until the required blood sample is collected. The heelstick procedure will end with the application of a Band-Aid by the laboratory technician. This is the standard approach to the heelstick procedure used at TCH. The research assistant will document the start and stop times of the heelstick procedure using a time-event marker in the data acquisition system.

Throughout the duration of the data collection period, the time, duration, and characteristic of all caregiving handling and significant environmental events will be recorded in the onsite computer database, including any nonpharmacologic comfort measures that might be provided by the caregiver before or during the heelstick procedure. Furthermore, if the infant experiences significant **physiologic** distress, all interventions performed by the caregiver to stabilize the infant will be recorded.

Following the heelstick observation period, the research assistant will complete the NONB (Als, 1984) and NTISS (Gray, et al., 1992) instruments using the patient's medical record. Data will also be collected on the number and types of noxious clinical procedures performed from the time of birth to the heelstick observation period using the infant's medical record. Data on time since last painful procedure will also be collected.

The diagram below illustrates the data collection procedures for the variables contained within this study:

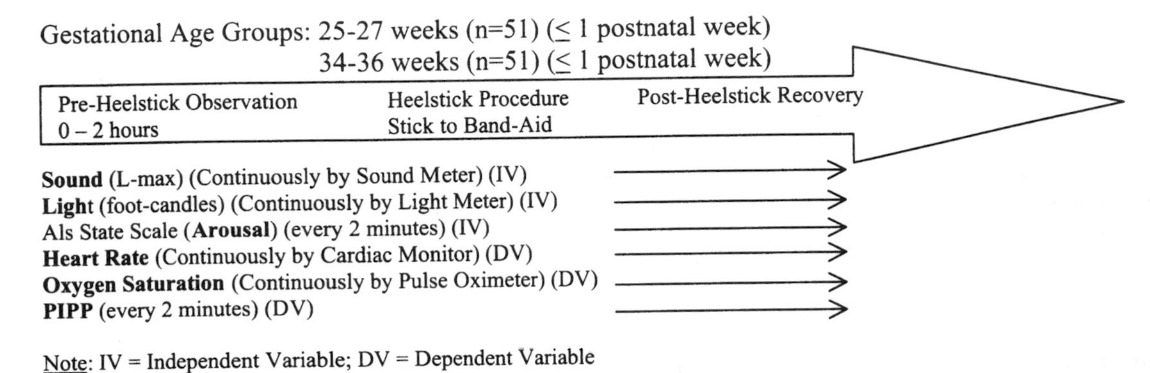

Figure 2. Data collection protocol.

Interrater Reliability: The reliability of the PI's and co-investigator's use of the Als State Scoring System has been estimated at greater than 0.85 with a national NIDCAP instructor (Linda Lutes, Sooner NIDCAP Training Center, Oklahoma City, Oklahoma). The PI will be responsible for ensuring that the research assistant is reliable in the Als State Scoring System before data collection.

Reliability of the PI's scoring the facial actions of the **PIPP** instrument was estimated at greater than 0.85 before data collection by an international expert in **pain responses** in infants (Bonnie Stevens, University of Toronto, Ontario, Canada). The PI will be responsible for ensuring that the co-investigator and research assistant are reliable in the **PIPP** instrument before data collection.

To further ensure reliability, ten percent of the observations (or $n = 10$) will be randomly selected for assessment of interrater reliability between study personnel using the Als State Scoring System as well as the **PIPP** instrument. Measurements of inter-rater reliability will occur beginning 10 minutes before the heelstick procedure through the first 10 minutes of the post-heelstick recovery observation period.

The PI received training in **physiologic** data acquisition during a Faculty Scientist Award from Emory University and is currently engaged in **physiologic** data collection and secondary analysis of **physiologic** variables during painful clinical procedures for a currently funded NIH research project entitled "Heart Rate Variability During Transition to Extrauterine Life" (Dr. M. Terese Verklan, Principal Investigator). In addition, Dr. Terese Verklan will be responsible for ensuring the reliability of the PI, co-investigator, and research assistant in **physiologic** data acquisition using the National Instruments Data Acquisition System before data collection. Furthermore, Carol Carrier will be responsible for ensuring that the PI and research assistant are reliable using the **sound** and **light** level meters before data collection.

Analysis:

Statistical analyses will be performed using the BMPD Program (Dixon, 1992). Descriptive statistics including frequencies and measures of central tendency and dispersion will be calculated for all demographic and study variables, as appropriate. For all analyses in this research, the level of significance will be $p \leq 0.05$. This analysis section will be organized by research questions and hypotheses.

1. What is the relationship between **sound** (as measured by a sound meter), **light** (as measured by a light meter), **arousal** levels (as measured by Als State Score) in the 2 hours preceding a heelstick procedure to:

    A. Immediate **physiological pain response** of preterm neonates to a heelstick procedure (as measured by **heart rate** and **oxygen saturation**)?

    B. Immediate **behavioral pain responses** of preterm neonates to a heelstick procedure (as measured by the **PIPP**)?

2. Is the relationship of **sound** (as measured by a sound meter), **light** (as measured by a light meter), **arousal** levels (as measured by Als State Score) in the 2 hours preceding a heelstick procedure moderated by **gestational age**?

Mixed model general linear models (GLMs) will be arranged with between-groups independent variables of **sound**, **light**, **arousal** levels, and **gestational age**; and one within-groups independent variable, occasion. A separate GLM will be used for each of the dependent variables, **heart rate**, **oxygen saturation**, and **PIPP**. Instead of a full factorial design, specific design terms will be developed: for Question 1, four two-way interactions will be tested (**sound, light, arousal**, and **gestational age** X occasion). Any significant 2-way interaction will be probed with simple main effects. For Question 2, three 3-way interactions will be built (**sound, light**, and **arousal** X **gestational age** X occasion). Any significant 3-way interaction will be decomposed into 2-way interactions and simple main effects to explain the effect.

3. Does variation in **sound** (as measured by a sound meter), **light** (as measured by a light meter), and **arousal** levels (as measured by Als State Score) in the 2 hours preceding a heelstick procedure predict:

    A. **Physiological disruption** from acute pain in preterm neonates (as measured by the **time for heart rate and oxygen saturation to return to baseline values).**

    B. **Behavioral disruption** from acute pain in preterm neonates following a heelstick procedure (as measured by **time for PIPP score to return to baseline value**).

Hierarchical regression analyses will be performed to examine the effect of **sound, light**, and **arousal** levels on **physiologic disruption** and **recovery time** of acute pain scores. The regression model will include three predictor variables (**sound** [mean Lmax value for preheelstick period], **light** [mean foot-candles value for preheelstick period], **arousal** level [mean of Als states 1-6 observed every two minutes during preheelstick period]). The dependent variables in the regression analyses are **time to return to baseline for heart rate, oxygen saturation and PIPP scores (recovery time**).

The centered main effects (**sound, light**, and **arousal**) will be tested first, followed by a test of cross-products (**gestational age** group by **sound, light**, and **arousal** levels). In separate regression analyses, dependent variables will be regressed on the three predictor variables (**sound, light**, and **arousal**). For all regression analyses, the environmental variables of **sound** and **light** will be entered first into the regression model as they are hypothesized to affect the third predictor, **arousal**. Multicollinearity will be assessed by examining the tolerance of all predictor variables, using the statistical program, BMPD-2R. Tolerances for predictor variables that fall below .40 will be excluded from further analysis. Furthermore, residual scatterplots will be obtained and inspected for multivariate outliers and to ensure that the assumptions for multiple regression have not been violated. Significant departures from normality will be handled by transforming affected variables to stabilize their variances.

4. Does **gestational age** interact with **sound** (as measured by a sound meter), **light** (as measured by a light meter), and **arousal** levels (as measured by Als State Score) in the 2 hours preceding a heelstick procedures in the prediction of:
   A **Physiological disruption** from acute pain in preterm neonates (as measured by the **time for heart rate and oxygen saturation to return to baseline values**).
   B **Behavioral disruption** from acute pain in preterm neonates following a heelstick procedure (as measured by **time for PIPP score to return to baseline value**).

Using BMDP-1R, a Chow test (test for equivalency of regression slope) will examine possible differences in regression planes between **gestational age** subgroups (25-27 weeks **gestational age** vs. 34-36 weeks **gestational age**). If the Chow test is nonsignificant, the regression analyses will be completed using the entire sample ($N = 102$). If the Chow test indicates group differences, separate regression slopes will be used to analyze the data.

Limitations of the Research:

The subjects are not randomly selected for the study; rather, their inclusion depends upon the availability of the parent(s) to sign a consent form and the willingness of the parent(s) to have their infant participate in the study.

Due to the very nature of clinical research, several factors may have an impact on the way in that data are collected. While the heelstick will be performed according to a standardized collection procedure, a number of different laboratory technicians may collect the blood. This, however, is a reflection of the actual practice infants experience. In addition the amount of blood to be collected may vary depending on the laboratory studies ordered and thus differences in the amount of time to collect blood is expected. Again, this is a reflection of the actual practice infants in the NICU experience. Also not all subjects will experience the same types of painful procedures or the same number of repetitions of the procedure during the first week of postnatal life. Since it would not be ethical to subject preterm infants to procedures they do not need, nor to withhold procedures they need just to ensure equivalence of experience, data will be collected on the number and type of painful procedures experienced until the heelstick is performed as well as the time since the last painful procedure.

Since infants will be cared for by different caregivers, it is possible that the infant's caregiver will provide additional nonpharmacologic comfort measures beyond the standardized comfort measure to be provided in this study. This again is a reflection of the actual practice infants experience. The research assistant will record nonpharmacologic comfort measures provided as well as a qualitative analysis of caregiving during data collection to identify caregiving factors she thinks are influencing infant responses.

Finally, one of the major problems in using data acquisition systems to collect **physiologic** measures is the voluminous amount of data that are collected. It is important to eliminate the unnecessary information coming from the analysis procedure and focus only on the pertinent information to answer the research question.

Timeline

	Year 01				Year 02			
	Qtr01	Qtr02	Qtr03	Qtr04	Qtr01	Qtr02	Qtr03	Qtr04
Order, set up equipment, program software for data acquisition	■							
Develop & refine on-line database	■							
Hire and train Research Assistant	■							
Data collection and data entry		■	■	■	■	■		
Data analysis				■	■	■	■	
Update literature review		■		■		■		■
Annual report				■				■
Final report								■
Manuscript preparation							■	■

Months: 0 3 6 9 12 15 18 21 24

E. Human Subjects

Sample

Every preterm infant admitted to the Newborn Care Center at TCH will be recruited for participation in a convenience sample of 102 infants who meet the following criteria: (a) infants between 25-27 weeks or 34-36 weeks **gestational age** at birth and appropriate for **gestational age** as determined by the New Ballard Score (Ballard, et al., 1991); (b) scheduled to receive a routine heelstick procedure within the first postnatal week. This subject inclusion criterion is demanded by the science of the research questions addressed.

Exclusion criteria include: a) chromosomal or genetic anomalies; b) significant central nervous system abnormality including seizures or a Grade III/IV intraventricular hemorrhage; c) infants born to mothers with a known history of substance abuse; d) infants who receive paralytic, analgesic, or sedating medications within 24 hours before the heelstick procedure.

Recruitment of Minority Subjects

In 1999, the racial composition of neonatal patients for the respective age groups at TCH is 22% African American; 29% Hispanic; 47% Caucasian; and 2% Other. The sample composition for this study is expected to be similar. Since the sample population is approximately evenly divided among minority versus non-minority groups, if more than one infant is available for inclusion in the study on any given laboratory collection day, preference will be given to infants of the youngest **gestational age**. If more than one infant meets the youngest **gestational age** criteria, preference will be given to recruitment of minority background. The rationale for choosing the youngest subjects as first preference is that there is a smaller pool of infants between 25-27 weeks **gestational age** than 34-36 weeks **gestational age**, making it more difficult to recruit this age sample. The rationale for recruiting minorities is to ensure adequate minority representation, since there will be equipment limitations. The recruitment goal for minority representation is that at least 50% of the sample will have a minority background. This percentage represents the actual minority representation at TCH. Recruitment will be reviewed monthly regarding minority inclusion.

Sources of Research Material

Once informed consent has been obtained from the parent(s), demographic data will be obtained from the medical record in order to complete the Neonatal Therapeutic Intervention Scoring System and Naturalistic Observation of Newborn Behavior Instruments. **Physiologic** data (**heart rate, oxygen saturation**) will be recorded continuously from cables connected to the infants' physiological monitor (SpaceLabs Cardiorespiratory Monitor with Nellcor Pulse Oximeter module). **Sound** and **light** levels will be collected using a Quest Technologies Sound Meter and Extech Light Meter, respectively. In addition, the research assistant will use bedside observation to measure the neonate's **arousal** level (Al's State Scoring System) as well as the **behavioral** components of the **PIPP** score (brow bulge, eye squeeze, nasolabial furrow). Data from all instruments will be recorded simultaneously using an on-site study computer.

Recruitment of Subjects

The Site Coordinator will make daily rounds to determine infants who meet eligibility criteria to participate in the study. Upon identification of a potential subject, the Principal Investigator or Site Coordinator will contact the parent(s) to set up an appointment to discuss the study and request informed consent. If the parent(s) agree to allow their infant to participate, they will be asked to sign a consent form. Those who sign the consent form will be given a copy to keep. A copy of the consent form will also be placed in the infant's medical record. Once 51 infants have been enrolled in each age group, subject recruitment will be halted for that respective group. To assure protection of rights of human subjects, approval to conduct the study is pending from the Institutional Review Boards of UTMB, TCH, and Baylor College of Medicine.

Potential Risks

The study proposed is repeated measures, naturalistic design; no additional procedures affecting the neonate or presenting any clinical risks are being proposed. There is, however, a potential risk of violation of confidentiality of the infant.

Protection Measures to Reduce Risks

All infants admitted into the study will be given a code number, and only the code number will appear on computer data files and data collection records. Data collection will be monitored by the principal investigator and site coordinator to ensure safety of the subjects.

Potential Benefits

The study may provide new information of how **sound, light,** and **arousal** levels influence the infant's ability to respond to and recover from painful procedures. This knowledge may improve assessment of pain in critically ill preterm neonates. Moreover, this improved understanding will permit caregivers to develop interventions to modify the NICU micro-environment in a manner that minimizes infant acute **physiologic** and **behavioral responses** to pain and thereby helps to decrease long-term neurobehavioral sequelae of chronic, repetitive pain experiences.

F Vertebrate Animals

Not Applicable

G Literature Cited

Als, H. (1984). *Manual for the naturalistic observation of newborn behavior (preterm and fullterm infants)*. Boston: Author.

Als, H. (1986). A synactive model of neonatal behavioral organization: Framework for the assessment of neurobehavioral development in the premature infant and for support of infants and parents in the neonatal intensive care environment. *Physical & Occupational Therapy in Pediatrics, 6*(3/4), 3-55.

Als, H., Lawhon, G., Brown, E., Gibes, R., Duffy, F., McAnulty, G., & Blickman, J. (1986). Individualized behavioral and environmental care for the very low birth weight preterm infant at high risk for bronchopulmonary dysplasia: Neonatal intensive care unit and developmental outcome. *Pediatrics, 78* 1123-1132.

Anand, K. (1997). Long-term effects of pain in neonates and infants. In T. S. Jensen, J. A. Turner, and Z Wiesenfeld-Hallin's (Eds.) *Proceedings of the 8th World Congress on Pain, Progress in Pain Research and Management (Vol. 8)*. Seattle: IASP Press.

Anand, K. (1998). Clinical importance of pain and stress in preterm neonates. *Biology of the Neonate, 73* 1-9.

Anand, K., Phil, D., & Hickey, P. (1987). Pain and its effects in the human neonate and fetus. *New England Journal of Medicine, 317*, 1321-1329.

Anand, K., Phil, D., Grunau, R., & Oberlander, T. (1997). Developmental character and long-term consequences of pain in infants and children. *Child and Adolescent Psychiatric Clinics of North America, 6*, 703-724.

Andrews, K., & Fitzgerald, M. (1994). The cutaneous withdrawal reflex in human neonates: sensitization, receptive fields, and the effects of contralateral stimulation. Pain, 56, 95-101.

Appleton, S. (1997). Handle with care: An investigation of the handling received by preterm infants in intensive care. *Journal of Neonatal Nursing, 3*, 23-27.

Ballantyne, M., Stevens, B., McAllister, M., Dionne, K., & Jack, A. (1999). Validation of the premature infant pain profile in the clinical setting. *Clinical Journal of Pain, 15*(4), 297-303.

Ballard, J., Khoury, J., Wedig, K., Wang, L., Eilers-Walsman, B. & Lipp, R. (1991). New Ballard Score expanded to include extremely premature infants. *The Journal of Pediatrics, 119*, 417-423.

Barker, D. & Rutter, N. (1995). Exposure to invasive procedures in newborn intensive care unit admissions. *Archives of Disease in Childhood, 72*, F47-F48.

Beaver, P. (1987). Premature infants' response to touch and pain: Can nurses make a difference? Neonatal Network, 6, 13-17.

Blackburn, S. & Patterson, D. (1991). Effects of cycled light on activity state and cardiorespiratory function in preterm infants. *Journal of Perinatal-Neonatal Nursing 4*(4), 47-54.

Bozzette, M. (1993). Observation of pain behavior in the NICU: An exploratory study. Journal of Perinatal & Neonatal Nursing, 7(1), 76-87.

Campos, R. (1989). Soothing-pain-elicited distress in infants with swaddling and pacifiers. Child Dev, 60, 781-792.

Carli, G., Montesano,, A., Rapezzi, S., & Paluffi, G. (1987). Differential effects of persistent nociceptive stimulation on sleep stages. *Behavioural Brain Research, 26*, 89-98.

Cooper-Evans, J. (1991). Incidence of hypoxaemia associated with caregiving in premature infants. *Neonatal Network, 10*, 17-24.

Corff, K., Seideman, R., Venkataraman, P., Lutes, L., & Yates, B. (1995). Facilitated Tucking: A nonpharmacologic comfort measure for pain in preterm neonates. *Journal of Obstetric, Gynecologic, and Neonatal Nursing, 24*, 143-147.

Craig, K., Whitfield, M., Grunau, R., Linton, J.,& Hadjistavropoulos, H. (1993). Pain in the preterm neonate: behavioral and physiological indices. Pain, 52, 287-299.

Dixon, W.J. (Ed.) (1992). *BMDP Statistical Software Manual.* Berkeley, CA: University of California Press.

Duxbury, M., Henly, S., Broz, L., Armstrong, G., Wachdorf, C. (1984). Caregiver disruptions and sleep of high-risk infants. *Heart and Lung, 13*, 141-147.

Fanconi, S. (1988). Reliability of pulse oximetry in hypoxic infants. *The Journal of*

Field, T., & Goldson, E. (1984). Pacifying effects of nonnutritive sucking on term and preterm neonates during heelstick procedures. *Pediatrics, 74*, 1012-1015.

Fitzgerald, M. & Anand K. (1993). Developmental neuroanatomy and neurophysiology of pain. In N. Schechter, C. Berde, & M. Yaster (Eds.), *Pain in infants, children, and adolescents* (pp. 11-31). Baltimore: Williams & Wilkins.

Fitzgerald, M., Millard, C., & McIntosh, N. (1989). Cutaneous hypersensitivity following peripheral tissue damage in newborn infants and its reversal with topical anaesthesia. Pain, 39, 31-36.

Fitzgerald, M., Shaw, A., MacIntosh, N. (1988). The postnatal development of the cutaneous flexor reflex: A comparative study in premature infants and newborn rat pups. *Developmental Medicine and Child Neurology, 30*, 520-526.

Franck, L. & Gregory, G. (1993). Clinical evaluation and treatment of infant pain in the neonatal intensive care unit. In N. Schechter, C. Berde, & M. Yaster (Eds.), Pain in infants, children, and adolescents (pp. 519-535). Baltimore: Williams & Wilkins.

Gadeke, R., Doing, B., Keller, F., & Vogel, A. (1969). The noise level in a children's hospital and the wake-up threshold in infants. *Acta Paediatrica Scandinavia, 58*, 164-170.

Gorski, P. (1983). Premature infants behavioral and physiological responses to care-giving interventions in the intensive care nursery. In J. Call, E. Gallenson, & R. Tyson (Eds.), *Frontiers of infant psychiatry* (pp. 256-263). New York: Basic Books, Inc.

Gorski, P. Hale, W., & Leonard, C. (1983). Direct computer recording of premature infants and nursing care: Distress following two interventions. *Pediatrics 72*, 198.

Gottfried, W. (1985). Environment of newborn infants in special care units. In A. Gottfried & J. Gaiter (Eds.), *Infant stress under intensive care: Environmental neonatology* (pp. 23-54). Baltimore: University Park Press.

Gray, J., Richardson, D., McCormick, M., Workman-Daniels, K., & Goldmann, D. (1992). Neonatal therapeutic intervention scoring system: A therapy-based severity-of-illness-index. *Pediatrics, 90*, 561-567.

Grunau, R. & Craig, K. (1987). Pain expression in neonates: Facial action and cry. *Pain, 28*, 395-410.

Grunau, R., Whitfield, M., & Petrie, J. (1994). Pain sensitivity and temperament in extremely low-birth-weight premature toddlers and preterm and full-term controls. *Pain, 58*, 341-346.

Grunau, R., Whitfield, M., Petrie, J., & Fryer, E. (1994). Early pain experience, child and family factors, as precursors of somatization: A prospective study of extremely premature and fullterm children. *Pain, 56*, 353-359.

Hicks, R., Coleman, D., Ferante, F., Sahatjian, M., & Hawkins, J. (1979). Pain thresholds in rats during recovery from REM sleep deprivation. *Perceptual and Motor Skills, 48*, 687-690.

Hicks, R., Moore, J., Findley, P., Hirshfield, C., & Humphrey, V. (1978). REM sleep deprivation and pain thresholds in rats. *Perceptual and Motor Skills, 47*, 848-850.

Hintze, J. (2000). *PASS 2000 User's Manual.* Kaysville, UT: NCSS, INC.

Holditch-Davis, D. & Calhoun, M. (1989). Do preterm infants show behavioral responses to painful procedures? In S. Funk, E. Tornquist, M. Champagne, et al., (Eds.), *Key aspects of comfort: Management of pain, fatigue, and nausea* (pp. 35-43). New York: Springer.

Holditch-Davis, D. (1990). The effect of hospital caregiving on preterm infants' sleeping and waking states. In S. Funk, E. Tornquist, M. Champagne, et al., (Eds.), *Key aspects of recovery: Improving nutrition, rest, and mobility* (pp. 110-122). New York: Springer.

Holditch-Davis, D. (1998). Neonatal sleep-wake states. In C. Kenner, J. Lott, & A. Flandermeyer's (Eds.), *Comprehensive neonatal nursing: A physiologic perspective (pp. 921-938).* Philadelphia: W.B. Saunders.

Johnston, C. & Stevens, B. (1996). Experience in a neonatal intensive care unit affects pain response. Pediatrics, 98(5), 925-930.

Johnston, C., Stevens, B., Franck, L., Jack, A., Stremler, R., & Platt, R. (1999). Factors explaining lack of response to heel stick in preterm newborns. JOGNN, 28(6), 587-594.

Johnston, C., Stevens, B., Yang, F., & Horton, L. (1995). Differential response to pain by very premature neonates. Pain, 61, 471-479.

Johnston, C., Stremler, R., Stevens, B., & Horton, L. (1997). Effectiveness of oral sucrose and simulated rocking on pain response in preterm neonates. Pain, 72, 193-199.

Jorgensen, K. (1993). *Developmental care of the premature infant: A concise overview.* S. Weymouth, USA: Developmental Care Division of Children's Medical Ventures.

Krechel, S. and Bildner, J. (1995). CRIES: A new neonatal post-operative pain measurement score: Initial testing of validity and reliability. Paediatric Anaesthesia, 5(1), 53-61.

Lenz, E., Pugh, L., Milligan, R., Gift, A., & Suppe, F. (1997). The middle-range theory of unpleasant symptoms: An update. *Advances in Nursing Science, 19*(3), 14-27.

Long, J., Lucey, J., & Philips, A. (1980). Noise and hypoxemia in the intensive care nursery. *Pediatrics, 65*, 143-145.

Lotas, M. & Walden, M. (1996). Individualized developmental care for very low-birth-weight infants: A critical review. *Journal of Obstetric, Gynecologic, and Neonatal Nursing, 25*, 681-687.

Mann, N., Haddow, R., Stokes, L., Goodley, S., & *Rutter*, N. (1986). Effect of night and day on preterm infants in a newborn nursery: Randomised trial. *British Medical Journal, 293*, 1265-1267.

Marchette, L., Main, R., Redick, E., et al. (1991). Pain reduction interventions during neonatal circumcision. Nursing Research, 40, 241-244.

McIntosh, N., Van Veen, L, & Brameyer, H. (1994). Alleviation of the pain of heel prick in preterm infants. Archives of Disease in Childhood, 70, F177-F181.

Miller, H. & Anderson, G. (1993). Nonnutritive sucking: Effects on crying and heart rate in intubated infants requiring assisted mechanical ventilation. Nursing Research, 42, 305- 307.

Murdoch, D. & Darlow, B. (1984). Handling during neonatal intensive care. *Archives of Disease in Childhood, 59*, 957-961.

National Commission to Prevent Infant Mortality. (1990). *Troubling trends: The health of America's next generation*. Washington, DC.

Norris, S., Campbell, L., & Brenkert, S. (1982). Nursing procedures and alterations in transcutaneous oxygen tension in premature infants. *Nursing Research, 31*, 330-336.

Owens, M. & Todt, E. (1984). Pain in infancy: Neonatal reaction to a heel lance. Pain, 20, 77-86.*Pediatrics, 112*, 424-427.

Peters, K. (1992). Does routine nursing care complicate the physiologic status of the premature neonate with respiratory distress syndrome? *Journal of Perinatal-Neonatal Nursing 6*(2), 67-84.

Pohlman, S. & Beardslee, C. (1987). Contacts experienced by neonates in intensive care environments. *Maternal -Child Nursing Journal, 16*, 207-226.

Shiao, S. Chang, Y., Lannon, H., & Yarandi, H. (1997). Meta-analysis of the effects of nonnutritive sucking on heart rate and peripheral oxygenation: Research from the past 30 years. Issues in Comprehensive Pediatric Nursing, 20, 11-24.

Shiroiwa, Y., Kamiya, Y., & Uchiboi, S. (1986). Activity, cardiac and respiratory responses of blindfold preterm infants in a neonatal intensive care unit. *Early Human Development, 14*, 259-265.

Slevin, M., Farrington, N., Duffy, G., Daly, L., and Murphy, J. (2000). Altering the NICU and measuring infants' responses. *acta paediatr, 89*(5), 577-81.

Speidel, B. (1978). Adverse effects of routine procedures on preterm infants. *Lancet, 1*, 864-866.

Stevens, B. & Johnston, C. (1994). Physiological responses of premature infants to a painful stimulus. *Nursing Research 43*, 226-231.

Stevens, B., & Ohlsson, A. (1998). Sucrose in neonates undergoing painful procedures. Neonatal Modules of the Cochrane Data Base of Systematic Reviews, electronic 1-13.

Stevens, B., Johnston, C., & Horton, L. (1993). Multidimensional pain assessment in premature neonates: A pilot study. JOGNN, 22(6), 531-541.

Stevens, B., Johnston, C., & Horton, L. (1994). Factors that influence the behavioral pain responses of premature infants. Pain, 59, 101-109.

Stevens, B., Johnston, C., Franck, L., Petryshen, P., Jack, A., & Foster, G. (1999). The efficacy of developmentally sensitive interventions and sucrose for relieving procedural pain in very low birth weight neonates. Nursing Research, 48(1), 35-43.

Stevens, B., Johnston, C., Petryshen, P., & Taddio, A. (1996). Premature infant pain profile: Development and initial validation. *Clinical Journal of Pain, 12*, 13-22.

Stevens, B., Taddio, A., Ohlsson, A., & Einarson, T. (1997). The efficacy of sucrose for relieving procedural pain in neonates: A systematic review and meta-analysis. Acta Paediatrica, 86, 837-842.

U.S. Department of Health and Human Services. (1992). *Acute pain management in infants, children, and adolescents: Operative and medical procedures* (AHCPR Publication. No. 92-0020). Rockville, Maryland: Author.

Van Cleve, L., Johnson, L., Andrews, S., Hawkins, S., & Newbold, J. (1995). Pain responses of hospitalized neonates to venipuncture. *Neonatal Network, 14*, 31-36.

Walden, M. (1997). *Changes over six weeks in multivariate responses of premature neonates to a painful stimulus*. Unpublished doctoral dissertation, The University of Texas at Austin, School of Nursing, Austin.

Wolke, D. (1987). Environmental neonatology. *Archives of Disease in Childhood, 62*, 987-988.

Zahr, L., & Balian, S. (1995). Responses of premature infants to routine nursing interventions and noise in the NICU. *Nursing Research, 44*, 179-185.

H Consortium/Contractual Arrangements

Subcontract to Texas Children's Hospital, Houston, Texas.
Joan Smith, RN, MSN will serve at 5% effort as Site Coordinator for the project. She will assist the Principal Investigator in addressing staff questions related to the research project and in problem solving data collection issues as they arise. Ms. Smith will assist the Principal Investigator in subject recruitment by making daily rounds of newly admitted infants to the Newborn Center to determine potential infants who meet study eligibility requirements. She will also assist the Principal Investigator in obtaining informed consent from parent(s). Ms. Smith will participate as needed in data collection in conjunction with the Principal Investigator and Research Assistant. Finally, Ms. Smith will assist the Principal Investigator in data analysis, interpretation, and dissemination, particularly as it relates to her expertise in environmental sound and light in the NICU.

This subcontract is currently under negotiation. Completed documentation of this subcontract will be forwarded as soon as it is available.

I. Consultants

Jean Smithers, PhD, RN, CCNS is an Associate Professor at The University of Texas Health Science Center-Houston and_will serve as a data acquisition consultant to the project. Dr. Smithers is an expert in the neonatal cardiovascular physiology and behavioral state. She has numerous data-based contribution in peer-reviewed professional journals and has been the principal investigator and co-investigator for several well-funded clinical studies relating to fetal and neonatal care. She is currently the principal investigator on a NIH R01 in which she uses the Physiological Data Acquisition System by National Instruments (Austin, Texas) to examine heart rate variability and state transition of the fetus to neonate through the first 10 hours of life. She will provide consultation in computerized data acquisition of the physiologic variables in this study using the National Instruments data acquisition set-up. Upon completion of data collection, Dr. Smithers will assist in analysis and interpretation of the data. She will provide approximately two days of consulting services in Year 01 and four days of consultation in Year 02.

Jeanne Doe, RN, Ph.D., Professor and Associate Dean for Research at The University of Texas Medical Branch - Galveston will serve as a no-cost consultant for the project. She has served as a non-remunerated consultant to the principal investigator during the development of her preliminary studies leading to this study and in the development of this study. Dr. Doe brings expertise in many aspects including infant special care, research development, data management and NIH funding. She will provide ongoing guidance and advisement during the project period on the collection and management of data as well as during data interpretation in regard to clinical relevance.

APPENDIX

A. Dissertation manuscript submitted, *Changes Over Six Weeks in Physiologic and Behavioral Responses of Extremely Preterm Neonates to a Painful Stimulus*
B. Premature Infant Pain Profile (PIPP)
C. Als State Scoring System
D. New Ballard Score
E. Neonatal Therapeutic Intervention Scoring System
F. Naturalistic Observation of Newborn Behavior Instrument (NONB)
G. Letters of Support

Protocol Worksheet

Patient's Name: ____________________ Medical Record #: ________________
Hospital: _________________________

PREPARATION

_____ 1. NICU nurse identifies eligible infants on admission
   a. Performs New Ballard Score
   b. Ensures inclusion criteria are met (at birth)
      1. 24 - 26 weeks PCA at birth
      2. Continuous cardiac/oximeter monitoring
      3. Parent(s) able to read and write English or Spanish
      4. Parent(s) 18 years of age or older
      5. Expected scheduled heelsticks beginning by 27 weeks PCA
   c. Ensures infant does not meet exclusion criteria (at birth)
      1. Birth weight SGA/LGA
      2. Physical or neurologic congenital anomalies
      3. Abnormal neurologic signs or a Grade III/IV IVH
      4. Known fetal exposure to drugs of addiction
      5. Systemic analgesics, including narcotic and sedative agents, within 24 hours prior to data collection with evidence of low urine output (< 1 mL/Kg/Hour)

_____ 2. Nurse seeks permission of neonatologist to approach parent(s) with letter of information

_____ 3. Nurse reads letter of information to parent(s) and asks if they are willing to hear more about the study

_____ 4. Nurse informs principal investigator if parent(s) indicate an interest in hearing more about the study

_____ 5. Principal Investigator obtains permission of parent(s) for infant to participate in study

_____ 6. Principal Investigator gives parent(s) a copy of consent and places a copy in the infant's medical record

_____ 7. Principal Investigator confirms weekly eligibility criteria are met
   a. Routine weekly heel stick scheduled
   b. Continuous cardiac/oximeter monitoring
   c. Systemic analgesics, including narcotic and sedative agents, not given within the previous 24 hours prior to data collection (also urine output > 1 mL/Kg/Hour)

_____ 8. Principal Investigator informs laboratory/nursing of data collection time day prior to observation period

_____ 9. One hour prior to data collection, nurse performs care giving activities. The caregiver will first, change the infant's diaper, while research assistant scores the infant's response using the PIPP during the first 30 seconds for each 2 minute interval. For the data observation period, the infant will be dressed only in a diaper. The infant will be placed in the right lateral position with a Bendy Bumper.

_____ 10. Principal Investigator arranges bed/infant to maximize view of infant/monitor readings during data collection period

_____ 11. Principal Investigator confirms with laboratory technician/nursing scheduled time of heel stick procedure

_____ 12. Principal Investigator reminds nursery personnel that verbal communication and interruptions must be kept to a minimum during study

_____ 13. Principal Investigator posts sign, "Study in Progress. Please do not interrupt."

_____ 14. Principal Investigator randomizes heel for heel stick procedure

BASELINE

_____ 1. Study personnel position themselves closest to the infant's head.

_____ 2. Principal Investigator records behaviors every 2 minutes using BOS for 20 minutes.

_____ 3. At beginning of every 2 minute interval, the principal investigator will count the infant's respiration for 30 seconds.

_____ 4. Principal Investigator will record the heart rate and oxygen saturation at 30 seconds during each 2 minute period

_____ 5. Research assistant will score for the presence of brow bulge, eye squeeze, and nasolabial furrow during the first 30 seconds of each 2 minute interval.

_____ 6. The research assistant will score the PIPP during the first 30 seconds of each 2-minute interval.

_____ 7. Throughout the data collection periods, the Principal Investigator will continuously record environmental conditions (activity levels, noise, lighting levels).

_____ 8. Throughout the data collection periods, the research assistant will 1) maintain the infant in the side lying position; 2) remove all extraneous stimulation such as stroking, talking, position shifts, etc., 3) provide Bendy Bumper support to keep the infant's arms and legs in a flexed, midline position.

_____ 9. If the infant experiences, significant physiologic distress, the Principal Investigator will record all interventions performed by the caregiver to stabilize the infant. If the study must be halted, another observation period within the same week will be chosen.

Heelstick Procedure

_____ 1. After 20 minutes on the timer, the laboratory technician/research assistant will apply a heel warmer to the randomized heel.

_____ 2. Data will continue to be collected as described in baseline section.

_____ 3. At 22 minutes on the timer, the laboratory technician will perform the heel stick procedure according to standard protocol (have equipment open & ready to go).

_____ 4. The Principal Investigator will document the heel used, the number of heel lances and the start and stop times of the heel stick procedure on the BOS.

Recovery Period

_____ 1. Beginning with the time from the laboratory technician's last physical contact with the infant, Time 2 timer will be started and 20 minutes of observation will continue as described in the baseline section.

Post Data Collection Period

_____ 1. On each day of heel stick observation is performed, the Principal Investigator will complete the following instruments using the patient's medical record and interviewing the neonatologists and nurses when necessary.
   A. Naturalistic Observation of Newborn Behavior Instrument.
   B. Number of heel stick procedures performed from birth to each data collection period.
   C. Neonatal Therapeutic Intervention Scoring System

_____ 2. The infant will be foot-printed for the Certificate of Appreciation to be given to the parents following data collection at 32 weeks PCA.

Data Collection Periods

_____ 27 weeks (Date: __________ Time: ___________)
Technician: ______________________________

_____ 28 weeks (Date: __________ Time: ___________)
Technician: ______________________________

_____ 29 weeks (Date: __________ Time: ___________)
Technician: ______________________________

_____ 30 weeks (Date: _________ Time: __________)
Technician: ____________________________

_____ 31weeks (Date: __________ Time: __________)
Technician: ____________________________

_____ 32 weeks (Date: _________ Time: __________)
Technician: ____________________________

Other

_____ 1. 10% Assessment of Inter-rater reliability

Source: Walden, M. (1997). *Changes over Six Weeks in Multivariate Responses of Premature Neonates to a Painful Stimulus.* Unpublished doctoral dissertation, The University of Texas at Austin, School of Nursing, Austin.

AA

Form Approved Through 2/28/01
OMB No. 0925-0001

Department of Health and Human Services
Public Health Service

Grant Application

Follow instructions carefully.
Do not exceed character length restrictions indicated on sample.

LEAVE BLANK—FOR PHS USE ONLY.

Type	Activity	Number
Review Group		Formerly
Council/Board *(Month, Year)*		Date Received

1. TITLE OF PROJECT

2. RESPONSE TO SPECIFIC REQUEST FOR APPLICATIONS OR PROGRAM ANNOUNCEMENT ☐ NO ☐ YES *(If "Yes," state number and title)*
Number: Title:

3. PRINCIPAL INVESTIGATOR/PROGRAM DIRECTOR New Investigator ☐ YES

3a. NAME *(Last, first, middle)*

3b. DEGREE(S)

3c. SOCIAL SECURITY NO. ***Provide on Form Page KK.***

3d. POSITION TITLE

3e. MAILING ADDRESS *(Street, city, state, zip code)*

3f. DEPARTMENT, SERVICE, LABORATORY, OR EQUIVALENT

3g. MAJOR SUBDIVISION

3h. TELEPHONE AND FAX *(Area code, number and extension)*
TEL:
FAX:

E-MAIL ADDRESS:

4. HUMAN SUBJECTS ☐ No ☐ Yes

4a. If "Yes," Exemption no. or IRB approval date { ☐ Full IRB or ☐ Expedited Review

4b. Assurance of compliance no.

5. VERTEBRATE ANIMALS ☐ No ☐ Yes

5a. If "Yes," IACUC approval date

5b. Animal welfare assurance no.

6. DATES OF PROPOSED PERIOD OF SUPPORT *(month, day, year—MM/DD/YY)*
From | Through

7. COSTS REQUESTED FOR INITIAL BUDGET PERIOD
7a. Direct Costs ($) | 7b. Total Costs ($)

8. COSTS REQUESTED FOR PROPOSED PERIOD OF SUPPORT
8a. Direct Costs ($) | 8b. Total Costs ($)

9. APPLICANT ORGANIZATION
Name
Address

10. TYPE OF ORGANIZATION
Public: → ☐ Federal ☐ State ☐ Local
Private: → ☐ Private Nonprofit
Forprofit: → ☐ General ☐ Small Business

11. ORGANIZATIONAL COMPONENT CODE

12. ENTITY IDENTIFICATION NUMBER | Congressional District

DUNS NO. *(if available)*

13. ADMINISTRATIVE OFFICIAL TO BE NOTIFIED IF AWARD IS MADE
Name
Title
Address

Telephone
Fax
E-mail

14. OFFICIAL SIGNING FOR APPLICANT ORGANIZATION
Name
Title
Address

Telephone
Fax
E-mail

15. PRINCIPAL INVESTIGATOR/PROGRAM DIRECTOR ASSURANCE: I certify that the statements herein are true, complete and accurate to the best of my knowledge. I am aware that any false, fictitious, or fraudulent statements or claims may subject me to criminal, civil, or administrative penalties. I agree to accept responsibility for the scientific conduct of the project and to provide the required progress reports if a grant is awarded as a result of this application.

SIGNATURE OF PI / PD NAMED IN 3a. *(In ink. "Per" signature not acceptable.)* | DATE

16. APPLICANT ORGANIZATION CERTIFICATION AND ACCEPTANCE: I certify that the statements herein are true, complete and accurate to the best of my knowledge, and accept the obligation to comply with Public Health Service terms and conditions if a grant is awarded as a result of this application. I am aware that any false, fictitious, or fraudulent statements or claims may subject me to criminal, civil, or administrative penalties.

SIGNATURE OF OFFICIAL NAMED IN 14. *(In ink. "Per" signature not acceptable.)* | DATE

PHS 398 (Rev. 4/98) Face Page AA

DD Principal Investigator/Program Director *(Last, first, middle):* ______

DETAILED BUDGET FOR INITIAL BUDGET PERIOD DIRECT COSTS ONLY	FROM	THROUGH

PERSONNEL *(Applicant organization only)*					DOLLAR AMOUNT REQUESTED *(omit cents)*		
NAME	ROLE ON PROJECT	TYPE APPT. *(months)*	% EFFORT ON PROJ.	INST. BASE SALARY	SALARY REQUESTED	FRINGE BENEFITS	TOTALS
	Principal Investigator						
			SUBTOTALS →				

CONSULTANT COSTS		
EQUIPMENT *(Itemize)*		
SUPPLIES *(Itemize by category)*		
TRAVEL		
PATIENT CARE COSTS	INPATIENT	
	OUTPATIENT	
ALTERATIONS AND RENOVATIONS *(Itemize by category)*		
OTHER EXPENSES *(Itemize by category)*		
SUBTOTAL DIRECT COSTS FOR INITIAL BUDGET PERIOD		$
CONSORTIUM/CONTRACTUAL COSTS	DIRECT COSTS	
	FACILITIES AND ADMINISTRATION COSTS	
TOTAL DIRECT COSTS FOR INITIAL BUDGET PERIOD *(Item 7a, Face Page)* →		$

PHS 398 (Rev. 4/98) (Form Page 4) Page ______ DD

Number pages consecutively at the bottom throughout the application. Do not use suffixes such as 3a, 3b..

BUDGET FOR ENTIRE PROPOSED PERIOD OF SUPPORT
DIRECT COSTS ONLY

BUDGET CATEGORY TOTALS		INITIAL BUDGET PERIOD *(from Form Page 4)*	ADDITIONAL YEARS OF SUPPORT REQUESTED			
			2nd	3rd	4th	5th
PERSONNEL: *Salary and fringe benefits Applicant organization only*						
CONSULTANT COSTS						
EQUIPMENT						
SUPPLIES						
TRAVEL						
PATIENT CARE COSTS	INPATIENT					
	OUTPATIENT					
ALTERATIONS AND RENOVATIONS						
OTHER EXPENSES						
SUBTOTAL DIRECT COSTS						
CONSORTIUM/ CONTRACTUAL COSTS	DIRECT					
	F & A					
TOTAL DIRECT COSTS						

TOTAL DIRECT COSTS FOR ENTIRE PROPOSED PERIOD OF SUPPORT *(Item 8a, Face Page)*→ $

JUSTIFICATION. Follow the budget justification instructions exactly. Use continuation pages as needed.

Budget Justification: Year 01

Personnel

*__Kenner__ (15%) as program Director/Principal Investigator will be administratively responsible for al aspect sof the grant.

*__Smith__ (40%) as Investigator will be responsible for oversight of data collection and the educational sequences including coordination among the consultants and assisting Smithers with the development assessment of newborns and their follow-up. The College of Nursing and Health is contributing half of her time to this project.

*__Smithers__ (40%) as Investigator will be responsible for the development assessments of newborns and follow-up as well as assisting Smith. The College of Nursing and Health is contributing half of her time to this project.

*__Brown__ (5%) as Collaborative Investigator will be responsible for educational efforts both for the health care providers and high-risk mothers regarding effects alcohol abuse on the mother and child. The College of Nursing and Health is contributing half of her time to this project.

*University employment contracts are for 32 weeks.

BIOGRAPHICAL SKETCH

Provide the following information for the key personnel in the order listed on Form Page 2.
Photocopy this page or follow this format for each person.

NAME	POSITION TITLE

EDUCATION/TRAINING *(Begin with baccalaureate or other initial professional education, such as nursing, and include postdoctoral training.)*

INSTITUTION AND LOCATION	DEGREE *(if applicable)*	YEAR(s)	FIELD OF STUDY

RESEARCH AND PROFESSIONAL EXPERIENCE: Concluding with present position, list, in chronological order, previous employment, experience, and honors. Include present membership on any Federal Government public advisory committee. List, in chronological order, the titles, all authors, and complete references to all publications during the past three years and to representative earlier publications pertinent to this application. If the list of publications in the last three years exceeds two pages, select the most pertinent publications. **DO NOT EXCEED TWO PAGES.**

CHECKLIST

TYPE OF APPLICATION *(Check all that apply.)*

☐ NEW application. *(This application is being submitted to the PHS for the first time.)*

☐ REVISION of application number: ____________________
(This application replaces a prior unfunded version of a new, competing continuation, or supplemental application.)

☐ COMPETING CONTINUATION of grant number: ____________________
(This application is to extend a funded grant beyond its current project period.)

INVENTIONS AND PATENTS *(Competing continuation appl.only)*
☐ No
☐ Yes. If "Yes," ☐ Previously reported ☐ Not previously reported

☐ SUPPLEMENT to grant number: ____________________
(This application is for additional funds to supplement a currently funded grant.)

☐ CHANGE of principal investigator/program director.
Name of former principal investigator/program director: ____________________

☐ FOREIGN application or significant foreign component.

1. ASSURANCES/CERTIFICATIONS

The following assurances/certifications are made and verified by the signature of the Official Signing for Applicant Organization on the Face Page of the application. Descriptions of individual assurances/certifications begin on page 27 of Section III. If unable to certify compliance where applicable, provide an explanation and place it after this page.

•Human Subjects; •Vertebrate Animals; •Debarment and Suspension; •Drug-Free Workplace *(applicable to new [Type 1] or revised [Type 1] applications only)*; •Lobbying; •Delinquent Federal Debt; •Research Misconduct; •Civil Rights (Form HHS 441 or HHS 690); •Handicapped Individuals (Form HHS 641 or HHS 690); •Sex Discrimination (Form HHS 639-A or HHS 690); •Age Discrimination (Form HHS 680 or HHS 690); •Financial Conflict of Interest.

2. PROGRAM INCOME *(See instructions, page 19.)*
All applications must indicate whether program income is anticipated during the period(s) for which grant support is requested. If program income is anticipated, use the format below to reflect the amount and source(s).

Budget Period	Anticipated Amount	Source(s)

3. FACILITIES AND ADMINISTRATION COSTS (F & A)
Indicate the applicant organization's most recent F & A cost rate established with the appropriate DHHS Regional Office, or, in the case of forprofit organizations, the rate established with the appropriate PHS Agency Cost Advisory Office. If the applicant organization is in the process of initially developing or renegotiating a rate, or has established a rate with another Federal agency, it should, immediately upon notification that an award will be made, develop a tentative F & A cost rate proposal. This is to be based on its most recently completed fiscal year in accordance with the principles set forth in the pertinent *DHHS Guide for Establishing Indirect Cost Rates,* and submitted to the appropriate DHHS Regional Office or PHS Agency Cost Advisory Office. F & A costs will ***not*** be paid on foreign grants, construction grants, grants to Federal organizations, grants to individuals, and conference grants. Follow any additional instructions provided for Research Career Awards, Institutional National Research Service Awards, and specialized grant applications.

☐ DHHS Agreement dated: ____________________ ☐ No Facilities and Administration Costs Requested.

☐ DHHS Agreement being negotiated with ____________________ Regional Office.

☐ No DHHS Agreement, but rate established with ____________________ Date __________

CALCULATION* *(The entire grant application, including the Checklist, will be reproduced and provided to peer reviewers as confidential information. Supplying the following information on F & A costs is optional for forprofit organizations.)*

a. Initial budget period: Amount of base $ __________ x Rate applied __________ % = F & A costs (1) $ __________

b. Entire proposed project period: Amount of base $ __________ x Rate applied __________ % = F & A costs (2) $ __________

(1) Add to total direct costs from form page 4 and enter new total on Face Page, Item 7b.
(2) Add to total direct costs from form page 5 and enter new total on Face Page, Item 8b.

*Check appropriate box(es):
☐ Salary and wages base ☐ Modified total direct cost base ☐ Other base *(Explain)*
☐ Off-site, other special rate, or more than one rate involved *(Explain)*

Explanation *(Attach separate sheet, if necessary.)*:

4. SMOKE-FREE WORKPLACE
Does your organization currently provide a smoke-free workplace and/or promote the nonuse of tobacco products or have plans to do so?
☐ Yes ☐ No *(The response to this question has no impact on the review or funding of this application.)*

Pink Sheet

Title: "Modulation of Neonatal Pain by Intensive Care Unit Environment and Sleep State"

Principal Investigator: Dr. Marlene Walden

This study is a partial replication of a previous study (Walden, 1997) that measured premature infant responses to heelsticks using the PIPP and several physiological measures similar to those proposed in this pilot. The investigator wishes to repeat the study using better measures of NICU sound and light. The relationship between quality of sleep, environmental factors and infant's responses to pain are clinically relevant. Knowledge concerning these relationships in adults cannot be automatically transposed on premature infants.

(Reviewer # 1): The background, theoretical basis, review of literature (including prior work by the investigators) are nicely presented, extensive and relevant. The lack of significant findings in the 1997 study was attributed to a sample size (N=11) that was too small; yet the sample size proposed for this study is the same (N=13-2 lost to attrition = 11). The title of this pilot is somewhat misleading in that this study will not test cause-effect relationships between environment and sleep upon pain. Instead, this study proposes to examine relationships among behavioral and physiological responses to acute procedural pain with light and noise in the ICU and the infant's sleep stages 24 hours prior to the painful procedure. There are no comparisons between infants with different light/dark experiences or with different levels of environmental sound. Rather, a naturalistic design will be used wherein any differences in lighting or noise that occur in the natural course of events during each infant's stay in the NICU will be recorded and examined together with ongoing recordings of infant physiology, REM and state variables to see if any relationships exist. The instruments are clearly described and their validity and reliability (stability) are addressed. The table that describes all variables and the time line for repeated measures is valuable. This table shows that five physiological measures, REM, State, NICU noise and NICU light will be measured for the 24 hours prior to 4 heelsticks occurring at 28, 30, 32, and 34 weeks of post-conceptional age. Some variables will be measured continuously, some at specified intervals. For a total of 20 minutes that include time prior to, during and after each heelstick, ten PIPP scores of the infant will be recorded.

This will produce rather "dense" quantitative data for eleven infants. Given this information, the methods for data analyses are unclear. Relationships between physiological measures and state will be examined using correlational methods. This is reasonable, except that plans for treating the continuously measured physiological variables are not delineated, except to say that they would be categorized somehow. Furthermore, it is unclear whether these contingency tables would be constructed intraindividually or interindividually.

Since each infant will have data collected for the 24 hours prior to several heelstick episodes, pooling all data together for the contingency tables means that each infant would be counted four times. For the second and third research questions, all the biobehavioral infant measures and all the measures of NICU noise and light levels that were obtained in the preceding 24 hours will be compared to the PIPP scores per heelstick episode per infant. It is difficult to envision how this would be accomplished. The PIPP scores change over time before, during and after the heelstick. Ten PIPP scores will be obtained per infant per heelstick episode. The data analysis description speaks of a single PIPP score as the dependent variable. It is unclear which of the ten PIPP scores would be chosen as the single dependent variable for these RMANOVAs.

Furthermore, it is difficult to visualize a two level (age, PIPP) RMANOVA involving several hundred measures of a single ICU (noise, light) or infant (physiological or sleep or sate) variable for eleven infants. If some type of time series analyses, using RMANOVA, is planned, it is not described as such. If some sort of data reduction is planned for the measurements obtained for 24 hours, this is not clearly described either. Finally, there is not provision made for correcting the alphas given that at least nine RMANOVAs will be run. This project will use consulting services from both the biobehavioral and data management and analysis cores.

(Reviewer # 2) : The significance of the study is well documented in the literature review and the study is relevant to the Center. The design is appropriate. The sample size calculation is based on the literature described, and validity and reliability of the instruments addressed with the exception of the physiological measures. Several of these measures appear to be clinical measures such as the NONB, NBS, the NTISS and the Als State Scoring System. Are these tools sensitive enough to detect differences in change over time so that they might be used in an intervention study? If as the author describes, these neonates have frequent invasive procedures, how will the investigators be able to observe "normal" sleep wake patterns in the 24 hours prior to the heel stick? A data collection protocol is provided and helpful. Will the assumptions of the ANOVA be met with the quasi-experimental design?

Investigators: The Principal and Co-Investigators appear well qualified, by virtue of previous research experience, to conduct this study. Dr. Walden has done previous research involving the same variables and research questions as this pilot.

Human Subjects: Issues are not addressed for this Pilot. Presumably the cover statement for the entire grant proposal that all proposals will obtain IRB approval and minorities will be included applies here.

Gender/Minorities/Children: Since this study deals with premature infants, the exclusion of older subjects is scientifically acceptable. Provisions for equal representation by gender and ethnic minority are not described.

Budget: Expenses seem reasonable. The budget is recommended as requested.

Action: The pilot is scored in the good to very good range.

Source: Summary Statement Prepared by the Scientific Review Administrator of the Initial Review Group for National Institute of Nursing Research (NINR). The comments refer to an evaluation of one of the three pilot/feasibility studies within a Center Grant application submitted May, 1999.

Note on next step based on scientific review—An R15 Area Grant was submitted to NINR in September, 2000 using recommendations provided in this Summary Statement. Specific changes included title, increased sample size, and description of plans for inclusion of gender and ethnic minorities. Additionally, extensive revisions were made in the data analyses section to address reviewer concerns.

Grant Application Process Planning Tool (GAPPT)

Preliminary Development

Event/Action	Suggested Deadline
• Decide on problem of interest. • Define/specify variables of concern. • Start literature search and retrieval. Contract staff to set up research and retrieval services. • Meet with staff to arrange funding search if necessary.	6 to 8 months prior
• PI (and co-investigators, if appropriate) to meet with Associate Dean/Director and staff to plan grant application process and support to be provided.	6 months prior
• Complete literature search and retrieval.	5 to 6 months prior
• Meet with staff to identify and schedule (add to Process Planning Tool): • external and internal proposal reviews, • availability/appropriateness of templates, boilerplates and forms and • **deadlines** for application development/assembly.	
• Write 1 to 2 page precis (an abbreviated version) outlining project significance, long-term goals, specific aims (if possible), population(s), human subject involvement and tentative time line. • Begin process of identifying 3 to 4 well-know experts in content and methods areas as (1) potential proposal reviewers, and/or (2) consultants.	5 months prior
• Use precis as basis for meetings with clinical agencies, community groups agencies, etc. in arranging access to subjects/support:, If appropriate/relevant: • Offer template letter of support. • Collect information to describe performance site: resources and services to be available.	

Proposal Development and Review

Event/Action	Suggested Deadline
• Change precis to preliminary version of the research plan that includes background and significance, subject access, time line changes, methods summary. • Contact funding agency representative if not already done. Send proposal/precis if requested.	3 to 4 months prior

• Contact external reviewer(s): Obtain agreement and schedule review.
• Select, contact, and obtain agreement from consultants.
  • Discuss roles/responsibilities, periods/methods of contact/support and reimbursement.
  • Solicit letter of support and modular budget style biosketch, or information to construct one.
• Revise preliminary proposal to full Research Plan (A—D + G at least).
	3 months prior

• Send Research Plan to expert reviewer. • Work with staff and staff who collect specific costs for projected budget items. • Collect letters of support/agreement from agencies and consultants and own School, if appropriate. • Meetings with Director and staff about budget. Complete budget worksheet for staff, who will begin preparing the detailed budget. • Discuss faculty buyout(s) with chairperson(s).	2 to 3 months prior
• Staff follow-up (if necessary) to collect biosketch information for all key personnel. **Deadline for all CVs that need to be converted to biosketch format/template.** • Revise Research Plan on the basis of external reviewer comment. Add sections E, H and I. • Revise Research Plan to internal reviews (2 to 3 weeks prior to review).	2 months prior
• **Deadline for creation of budget spreadsheet (capped budget).** • **Deadline for graphics, complex tables to be created, or instruments to be formatted.** • Internal Review of proposal. • See template to prepare budget narrative.	1 month prior

• Finalize title and final changes to personnel. • Finalize Research Plan (A–I) on basis of Internal Review feedback. • Consortial/subcontractual agreements: get required forms and documents Consortial/subcontractual agencies. • Work with staff to finalize budget and budget narrative. Staff will check budget documents with designated School/College and University Research Office personnel. • Collect appendix material?staff for assembly and copying.	2 weeks to 1 month prior
• Add agency/other site information to Resources boiler-plate document and tailor to fit project. • Schedule transmittal signatures of chairperson and deans. • Write abstract?staff for "fit" and revision, if necessary. • Begin work on Institution Review Board protocol, if human subjects are involved.	2 weeks prior
• Deadline for Face Page Information. **• Deadline for Final version abstract (Form BB).** **• Deadline for Resources document.** **• Deadline for final Research Plan (A–I) to be formatted by staff.** **• Deadline for Budget Justification.**	1 week prior
• Deadline for Transmittal Form information. **• Deadline for Checklist information.** **• Deadline for appendix materials.** **• Deadline for Personal Data Form information.**	Deadline: 1 week prior
• Final PIs check for all application components, if not previously approved. • Write cover letter on letterhead?staff. • Obtain necessary signatures on Transmittal Form. • Staff will copy the application, and assemble and deliver all materials to the University Research Office.	Deadline: 1 week prior

Used with permission from Crain, H.C., and Broome, M.E. 2000. Tool for planning the grant application process. *Nursing Outlook* 48(6): 288–293.

Index

S

T